I0460462

His
Choosing

**Surrendering to the Unseen Forces That
Shape Our Lives**

Copy rights

Holy Bible, New International Version®, NIV® Copyright ©1973, 1978, 1984, 2011 by Biblica, Inc.® Used by permission. All rights reserved worldwide.

Holy Bible, New Living Translation, copyright © 1996, 2004, 2015 by Tyndale House Foundation. Used by permission of Tyndale House Publishers, Inc., Carol Stream, Illinois 60188. All rights reserved.

Scripture taken from the New King James Version®. Copyright © 1982 by Thomas Nelson. Used by permission. All rights reserved.

Copyright © 2015 by The Lockman Foundation, La Habra, CA 90631. All rights reserved.

The Holy Bible, English Standard Version. ESV® Text Edition: 2016. Copyright © 2001 by Crossway Bibles, a publishing ministry of Good News Publishers.

New American Standard Bible®, Copyright © 1960, 1971, 1977, 1995, 2020 by The Lockman Foundation. All rights reserved.

G4982 - sōzō - Strong's Greek Lexicon (kjv)

https://www.blueletterbible.org/lexicon/g4982/kjv/tr/0-1/

Copyright © 1954, 1958, 1962, 1964, 1965, 1987 by The Lockman Foundation

Copyright © 2021 by Discovery Bible.

www.troybrewer.com

Back cover photo: Lynell H. Smith Photography

Cover design and interior design was created by Erin May.

Editor: Bill Assini

Copyright © 2025 Erin May

All rights reserved.

ISBN: 979-8-9927638-0-5 (trade paperback) | ISBN: 979-8-9927638-1-2 (ebook)

DEDICATION

I dedicate this book to my amazing daughter Bryce.
Life is so much sweeter with you by my side.

CONTENTS

ACKNOWLEDGMENTS

God- Thank you for loving me. My life was a mess, and you made it into something beautiful.

Bill Assini- Thank you for coming alongside the creation of this book. Your editing skills and feedback were such a blessing!

Rachel Assini- Thank you for supporting and encouraging me all these years.

Mom- Thank you for encouraging me that God has a purpose for my pain.

Bryce May- My biggest cheerleader! You are an amazing girl, thank you for hearing my stories over-and-over again.

CHAPTER 1- WITNESS TO THE MIRACULOUS

Life-changing moments are rare. But when they do happen, it's a ripple effect. It doesn't just change one life. It affects all the lives around them.

I walked quickly towards the hospital. It was a warm morning due to the climate I was in. This hospital is nestled in the hot California desert. During this time of year, it wasn't a cool morning. The sun hadn't fully come up yet, and already a slight drip of sweat slid down the corner of my face.

It was my clinical rotation for the Respiratory Therapy program. I thought, "I am a student and cannot be late!" I walked into the break room, where the clinical instructor was handing out patient assignments. Relief hit me as I realized I made it. Now I could breathe.

I was paired with a middle-aged woman who had a lax mood about her. She was not particularly happy that morning. She glanced over at me as the instructor told her she would have a student today. I felt a little drawn back to see the disappointment on her face. I sat down in an empty chair. The room was small compared to the large brown table in the middle of the room.

The atmosphere soon filled with voices as reports were given. The night-shifter speaking to us had dark circles under both her eyes. I could tell she was ready to get some sleep after a long night.

My preceptor and I made our way to the critical patient side of the hospital. This was the ICU unit. Work began for us as we entered rooms one by one to take care of patients on our list for that day.

As we entered one room, I saw a man in his mid-twenties lying lifeless on the bed. I remembered him from a few days before. My memory flashed back when I was in the emergency room. That's when he first came in. Ambulance lights flashed as the EMS team rushed this man into an open ER room. As CPR was performed, reports were given out loud for all to hear in the room.

"This man was found down between a car and the curb. He is a drug overdose. Down-time was unknown," reported the paramedic.

The doctor yelled for another round of epinephrine. The room was chaotic. Everyone was working hard to save this 26-year-old man's life. Two minutes went by, and it was time to check for another pulse.

"We have a pulse doc," says the nurse.

Chest compressions were stopped. The man was placed on a ventilator as care continued. It was later in the hour I was ordered by the doctor to get an arterial blood sample. As I moved to the bedside, I pulled down the bed rale to get access to his left arm. And that's when I saw his arms and legs moving inward in a repetitious form. I asked the nurse what was happening.

"It looks like posturing," she said.

"What's that?" I asked.

"It's a sign of brain damage when the extremities move inward consistently like that," stated the nurse.

My flashback memory faded as I returned to the present. I heard the beeps and chimes in the room as there were monitors and machines everywhere. My preceptor stood next to me as she reported out loud that this man had no hope. Sadly, he was diagnosed as being brain-dead. The doctors at this point were trying to get the family to approve the patient to become an organ donor and ultimately cease care.

While my preceptor was still speaking to me, I heard another voice, "*I want you to pray for healing over this man.*" There was no confusion about whose voice that was. It was an all-too-familiar voice I had heard since I was a young girl.

It was God.

There was no doubt it was Him.

I felt compassion bubbling up from my heart. But I knew praying for him at that moment was not appropriate. The lady I was assigned with did not look like she was a woman of faith, and praying for your patients was not permitted.

We both left the room and walked to a computer. I opened the computer tab to start my charting on the patients we had just finished assessing.

In the span of thirty minutes to one hour, my preceptor with the lax attitude had a change in her mood. It looked like a premenopausal change in temperature by her fanning herself but escalated to her hyperventilating. She was having a panic attack. Calm words didn't help. And I soon realized she needed some medical assistance. I called my clinical instructor from her phone. Quick decisions were made to have her go to the emergency room.

After he had sent her away, he turned his head towards me. "Would you be able to check on the patients in the meantime?" he asked.

"Yes!" I said excitedly.

I knew God was doing something. He was creating a

window of opportunity to pray for the brain-dead man. My child-like faith rose inside me as I knew God was moving. He created a way where there was none. There was a short window of time when I was alone. I made my way to the patient's room. As I walked in, there was a tangible presence filling the air. It felt like a thick invisible cloud. I muttered, "God, you really do want to heal this man." I walked up to the patient and laid my hands on his chest. His lifeless body lay still under my hands.

With him being brain-dead, there was no brain activity to function and have any awareness of his surroundings. There was a ventilator breathing for him. Also, only a small percentage of his heart was working. I prayed a simple prayer out loud. I prayed for his brain, heart, and drug addiction. A Bible verse spilled out of my heart as I was praying, "The same Spirit that raised Jesus Christ from the dead lives in me," (Romans 8:11).

There was power in the room—a thickness in the air that could be sliced with a butter knife, if possible. The faith flowing out of me was so easy and light.

I leaned down to speak close to the man's ear, "Jesus is bringing you back from the dead! Jesus loves you so much he is bringing you back!". At this moment, the eyebrows on this man's face frowned as if he was trying to digest what I just said. With his eyes closed, he tilted his head towards me.

Did he just hear that?!

As I continued to pray for his healing, I made a mental note. *If I am feeling God's power, this man has to feel it because God is healing him!* He then began to move. I noticed his arms, legs, and head moving around. A few times he opened and closed his eyes.

Wow!

After I prayed, he went back to being comatose. The movement had stopped. The presence of God was still felt so powerfully in that room. There was a knowing inside me.

I knew God had healed him. The gift of faith was active in that place, and there was no doubt. I grabbed my clipboard and began writing numbers down to have for charting later. As I was writing his vitals, my hands were shaking. My whole body was shaking! All I could say repeatedly was, "Thank you Jesus, thank you Jesus, thank you Jesus." Thankfulness kept rolling out of my mouth. The presence of God left room for nothing else but the compelled need to worship and honor Him.

As I wrapped up my charting, I walked towards the door. An older man just so happened to be walking in. Our eyes met, and we both stopped in our footsteps. It was the patient's father. I smiled. He was a little hesitant with my mood due to our setting. And then I spoke, "God told me to pray for your son. Is that ok?"

"Yes, of course. There is a whole church congregation praying for him right now," said the father. There was grief on his face. But after making that statement, he tried his best to smile.

I didn't tell the father I had already prayed. I felt compelled to do it all over again. I placed my two hands on the patient's chest. I began to pray. The same prayer flowed out of me. I heard weeping from behind me. It was the father. I opened my eyes to see his son moving once again. After I prayed the second time, the patient went right back to being comatose. Again.

I looked at the father and joyfully stated, "God healed your son."

What did I just say?! It's one thing praying for a patient, but stating God supernaturally healed his son was a very bold statement, especially after his body went back to being comatose. My paperwork was gathered. I left the room.

I left full of faith and excited for what just took place. As I walked down the hallway, it was almost as if the gift of faith evaporated from my midst. The flowing power that filled the air was gone. And then a different voice intruded my thoughts. Different, knowing it wasn't me. Different, knowing it wasn't God.

You gave that father false hope. This patient is going to die, and you will be in big trouble. You will never graduate. You're going to fail school now! Your faith wasn't strong enough.

Walking down the hallway, I made a quick left to follow the signs for the bathroom. Thankfully, it was a single bathroom. I locked the door behind me. I sat down on the dirty floor with my back against the wall. I began to cry. Thoughts of failing God flooded my mind. *Why didn't this man completely wake up?* I pictured him being ready for the ET-tube to be pulled out! Eventually, I had to dry my tears and return to work.

My day finished. As I stepped out of the hospital into the now 115-degree air, my head was throbbing. I felt so exhausted. My demeanor was the opposite going out from that when I first came in. The young man I prayed for never woke up that day. He lay in his bed comatose.

The morning day presented me with such high hopes, the sun was rising over the east as I walked happily into my new future. Walking out that evening, I felt hopeless—the dreams of providing for my daughter as a single mom were crushed. My whole future was on the line.

The taunting thought repeated as I grabbed my key to unlock the car door. *You gave that father false hope.* This replayed in my mind as I drove home. Tears slowly fell as I prayed out loud, "But God, I heard you! Your presence was so powerful in that room! I feel like I failed you. I'm so sorry God."

His Timing, Not Mine

That evening, I typed a long email to a pastor at my church. In detail, I told the story as it unfolded. His voice. The window of opportunity. The power!

An email didn't take long to be returned. It was from my pastor. The response surprised me as I thought there would have been some judgment in his voice. He had a fatherly tone to his email as he responded with how proud he was I did what God told me to do. He encouraged me that the outcome wasn't in my hands; it was in God's. As I scanned to the end of the email, there was an exercise I was instructed to try. The exercise was to get in my quiet time with God and picture carrying his comatose body to the foot of the cross. Then, give him to Jesus.

That evening, I envisioned picking up this man and cradling him in my arms. I walked him up a hill. At the top of the hill, I laid him down at the foot of the cross. The cross that represents where Jesus sacrificed his own life. After giving God the outcome, I felt a load lift off my shoulders. I gave this man to Jesus.

The hospital prayer happened on a Monday, and my next clinical day was Friday. The night before my Friday clinical, I placed my headphones on and worshipped God. I rested in His unchanging goodness. No matter the outcome of this man's healing, I did what God told me to do. *Would the father be there? What would come of my career?*

Friday morning came quickly. I was paired up with a new preceptor for the day. I predicted this would happen since my other preceptor went to the ER earlier that week. As our day started, we walked by the room where the supernatural prayer took place. My heart rate increased a little. As his room came into view, I saw the head of the bed unusually raised higher than what was normal for someone who was on life-support. I then heard the audible hissing sound of a breathing treatment. As I scanned the room to take in the whole scene, I saw this man awake. His eyes were open. He turned his head in my direction as I stood in the doorway. God healed him!!

My preceptor told me, "The doctors can't explain it. This man just woke up." My overly excited answer was, "Oh wow, that's amazing!!" I was given a more detailed report. Midweek, he was taken off the ventilator and breathing on his own, two days after the supernatural prayer.

My faith had grown to a new level. I learned not to let my expectations cloud my judgment of what God wanted to do, especially HOW he chose to do it. I also knew that when the gift of faith and miracle-working power comes, I have supernatural faith to believe EVERYTHING God is doing and to lean on God's Word and promises when they lift. I needed to become stronger in that area.

1 Corinthians 12:7-10 NKJV
"But the manifestation of the Spirit is given to each one for the profit of all: for to one is given the word of wisdom through the Spirit, to another the word of knowledge through the same Spirit, to another faith by the same Spirit, to another gifts of healings by the same Spirit, to another the working of miracles, to another prophecy, to another discerning of spirits, to another different kinds of tongues, to another the interpretation of tongues."

Throughout the week, my heart was full of joy as I thought about God healing this man. God's Word is true! His healing miracles are still for today!

And then it hit me...

Why Not Me?

I stood facing the mirror. I was caught up in harming myself.

The episode started to invade my space once again. Anxiety had no mercy as it weighed down on my shoulders, giving me a harder time breathing. My hands were in self-destruction mode. My disorder of 18 years never left. It was still there. During that week, it slowly came back in full swing as I was locked in my episodes of self-destruction. It was obvious nothing had changed on my end. And then I prayed out loud, "Why didn't you heal me in that room?"

I stared at myself in the mirror, seeing my brokenness on display. There was no hiding from myself.

Silence.

Later that evening, I laid my Bible and notepad on my bed. I spent some time with God. I read his Word. I worshiped Him. Then, I started to ponder on the unique experience that took place. I remembered God using my hands to be a vessel to pray for the brain-dead man. And yet, I have been praying for years for my healing. Eighteen years! I believed God could heal me. *What was I missing? What was I doing wrong?*

I felt the gentle direction of the Holy Spirit guiding my heart. And then He spoke, "You have been asking the wrong questions... so you are waiting for the wrong response."

I sat there in silence.

This whole time, I believed God could heal me. But I always pictured Him healing me immediately. No hassle, no pain. But that was my problem. I allowed my mind to create an image of what I thought my healing should look like. *Was my own thinking keeping me from healing?* I started to think about how the man in the hospital was healed. I envisioned him waking up immediately. People shouting, "He's healed!" The doctors run in, puzzled by the commotion to see the man they clinically diagnosed as brain-dead to being instantly healed.

I felt led to look through the Bible that evening. As I turned through the pages of the New Testament, I saw Jesus' ministry on healing. There was no common theme to how people were healed. It was in His choosing. It was in His timing. It was in His ways. I then realized something. God's healing power flowed through my body. The room was filled with His presence to heal. My heart melted in humility. As I sat in the presence of God who sees and knows everything. *Who am I to argue with Him?* The tools and resources I've tried over the years did not work.

A thought turned into an open prayer, "I surrender God. Please forgive me for not listening to what you want to do in my life. You do whatever you want to me. You heal me in whatever way you see fit. You are God, and I am not."

Something changed within me after that supernatural encounter. I saw God's miracle-working power. I could trust Him.

Yes, don't give up Erin. God still heals today.

CHAPTER 2- TRAPPED IN DOING THINGS I HATE

Do you want to know a secret about me? I hurt myself. Not once. But over and over again. I strip myself of beauty – with my own two hands. Instead of building myself up, I spend hours destroying what God has designed me to be. Instead of hands that build, my hands destroy.

I remember the first time I did it like it was yesterday. I was only nine years old. I was drawing a picture at my grandma's dining room table. The clock was ticking in the background, alerting me as every boring second passed. I rubbed my eye. Something was irritating it. I gently moved my eyelashes between my fingertips. An eyelash was accidentally pulled out. Something strange happened. I stood and walked to the mirror next to the dining table. I leaned in close. I rubbed the eyelashes again—a slight tug. Another hair pulled out. I didn't know my life changed at that moment.

Over time, I would constantly have the urge to touch my eyelashes. The sensations would build up, and then a release would happen when another hair was pulled out. It felt like a reward.

My mom was helping me get ready for bed one evening. She asked me why I was doing it. I told her it felt good. She didn't understand what I meant. Her reasoning was I must be doing it to get attention. I was the youngest of three siblings. She told me to stop. The hair-pulling did not stop. I had a small gap of eyelashes missing over time. This turned into a more significant gap. I would alternate pulling from my right and left eyelid. Eventually, I pulled out all my eyelashes. All of them.

One morning, I was standing in the bathroom. A thought popped up in my mind.

You should just pull out a couple of eyebrow hairs. That way your eyelashes can start to grow back.

I leaned in close to the mirror, studied my eyebrows, grazed my finger, and shifted hairs out of place. Found a dark thick brow buried under, then pulled it out. The search was repeated. Again. And again.

Just one more hair.

Ok! This is the last one.

Just one more hair.

The urge to pull followed me throughout the day. What began to happen was my hands would rise to the pulling spots without me thinking. What began as a mistake, turned into a habit. Then, it developed into a hair-pulling disorder.

My school was getting harder. Kids noticed. I would wear sunglasses on the school bus to hide the hair-loss damage. One boy noticed me wearing them, even on rainy days. He began to make fun of me. "Hey, so why are you always wearing sunglasses? Did your dad beat you?" the little boy scoffed. The teasing on the bus became a regular event throughout the school year. This was the first wave of an ocean full of water. Water stored up for being teased, mocked, intentionally left out, stared at, and having my name crafted as a joke. Each wave that crashed against me left me more broken.

Losing It All

A couple of years later, that same irritating voice I had heard as a child returned to me. I did not know it was a demonic voice. I was at home, trapped in an episode of pulling out eyelashes and eyebrows when another thought flew into my head as if a little birdie sent it from afar.

You should pull out just a few hairs on your head. You have so much hair. No one will notice. Then your eyelashes and eyebrows can grow back.

The same repetitious scenario took place over the months. The hair-pulling increased, and the duration of the episodes increased. The number of hairs that fell all over me and the ground multiplied. I was in a downward spiral of torment. Every day I pulled out my hair. My sixth-grade year was a year I could never forget. This was the most challenging year of my life. The teasing continued. The longer I battled the disorder, the more broken I became.

My soul wounds grew deeper and deeper.

The waves continued to crash against me. My home life was difficult. There wasn't any support for what I was experiencing. My mother was a single mom who worked a lot. My grandma cared for my two older siblings and me when my mom was away.

The balding on my head grew, making it more challenging to hide. The primary targeting sites for pulling were on the sides of my head. It reached a point where I had a very thin flap of hair hiding the huge growing shame underneath. If I moved my head a certain way, the baldness would show. There was no hiding it anymore. I was going to school every day with huge bald spots on display for all the kids to laugh at.

"Erin, we need to talk," said my mom.

Walking from the hallway into the dining area, I saw my mom standing with her friend Julie. They have been friends for many years. It was at Julie's prompting from my appearance that she had a private discussion with my mom that something needed to change.

"Can you sit down with us?" my mom said.

As they both had motherly concerns on their faces, they agreed it was best that I shave my head since there wasn't much hair left. I began to weep. It was hard for me to let go of what I had. It was my hair, even though it was little. My brother overheard the chatter and ran into the room excitedly.

"I'll shave her head!"

I cried more.

I stood up and walked with my brother into the bathroom. I heard his electric shaver buzzing, and my hair was taken off. After he left the bathroom, I looked in the mirror. I had no hair. I was a girl. I was supposed to have hair. I cried again.

Survival Mode

A wig was purchased at a beauty store in town. It was a short bulky blonde wig. It was itchy. I did not like it. Going to school the first day wearing that new wig brought dirty looks and teasing all over again. Waves beating against my worth, my value. The stress grew at home as my mother carried the burden of being a single mom. Her concerns for me were jumbled up with threats to take away my bike or other belongings if she saw new missing hair. There were threats of discipline now. This was new for me since battling hair-pulling.

Walking on school grounds, I would just randomly roam around until the bell would ring. I saw kids playing handball at lunch one day. Curious, I walked up next to where they were. I was hoping to play. As I got close, a boy purposely threw the ball against my head. It throbbed as he and his friends laughed. Another time, two girls interlocked their arms and skipped by me. They were singing. The melody was a catchy song on the radio. But they changed the lyrics to mock my appearance.

A shift happened to me in 6th grade. I didn't feel safe at school. I didn't feel safe at home. A sense of belonging was covered by a dark cloud of grief and shame. *No one loves me. No one truly wants me.*

Bathrooms became a hideout spot for me. At recess and lunch, I would go into a bathroom stall and sit on the toilet. I would wait there until I heard the bell ring. Then, I would come out of hiding and head to class. This routine became normal for me. I was in survival mode. I was trying to make it through the day. Make it through one hour. Make it through one minute. The teasing was lessened. Talk was limited during class hours.

A Better Voice

I slammed the bathroom door and locked it. Dropped my backpack on the floor and sat on the dirty toilet with my clothes still on. I didn't care. My life was worse than what was on that seat. Tears flowed. I heard the main door open. A girl walked in. The gasps of crying changed to whispers as I tried to hold in my pain. I placed my hand over my mouth to try to muffle the crying. Within minutes, I heard the water turn on and the paper towel dispenser move. The large door leading to the playground shut. Silence. I was alone. I began to cry out loud again. I was so exhausted. So miserable trying just to survive every day. I prayed. "God! You can heal me. I know you can." The crying continued. I leaned my head against the side of the bathroom stall. "Please God help me, please help!" I continued.

As I was praying out loud, I heard a voice from within. I knew it wasn't my own because the voice was interrupting me while speaking. God spoke to me, "Erin, you will help people one day." Weeping stopped. My breathing started to slow with only a few quick gasps.

"I will?" I asked.

He didn't speak after that. But peace filled that bathroom stall. It was a comfort that I needed in that place at that moment.

Psalm 138:8
"The LORD will perfect that which concerns me; Your mercy, O LORD, endures forever; do not forsake the works of Your hands."

CHAPTER 3- BITTERNESS

"Unforgiveness is like a poison and a bitterness in your soul, and your life will always be bitter until you get rid of that poison," Joyce Meyer.

Having my hair-pulling disorder on top of becoming a teenager made things more challenging. In middle school, I was forming into the identity of what the world would call a nerd. My pant legs would rise to my high calf while sitting in class. My walk from classes changed. My head dropped lower. My mind conformed to this identity I was in. I felt like a nerd, so I walked like one.

My soul was screaming at me in pain. But I didn't know why. And living life with this disorder made it even worse. I didn't feel normal. I felt like an outcast, a kid who got the short end of the stick. Some kids at school tried to be nice to me. But I was in a deep darkness of bitterness, and it was hard to get out. It was like I had a shovel and kept digging myself into a deeper and deeper hole. Each week in middle school, a depth of bitterness and unforgiveness grew.

Hope Deferred

In 7th grade, I was home one evening with my mom. She called me into her room. She said, "Erin, I heard of someone who can pray for healing over you."

My heart skipped a beat in hope. As I looked at my mom, she had a determination on her face that this may work. "Who is it Mom?" I asked.

"It's a lady in Las Vegas; she is a nun. She has a reputation of praying over people, and they get healed." A glimmer of hope filled my heart. My torment could end, and I could finally start to be happy.

My mom dialed the number and spoke briefly to the woman on the other line. She handed the phone to me, and I heard the voice of one who had the strength of God to heal me. The nun prayed for me over the phone. She prayed for healing and that I would get all my hair back.

I lay in bed that night with the bed covers grasped in my hands. My heart was hurting. But I chose to believe, to have faith in God, that he is my healer. I determined in my heart that I believed all my eyelashes would be grown back by morning. "I believe in you, God. I know you healed me," I prayed before falling asleep.

The following day, my drowsy eyes began to open from my deep sleep.

It took a few minutes, but then my memories quickened to the powerful prayer the other night. I jumped out of bed and made my way to the bathroom. I had faith that God had healed me and given me back my hair. My heart was like a ship headed to clear waters—the hopes of clear blue skies and beautiful sunsets. Staring in the mirror, I saw my bare eyelids. My heart sank. As I glanced at myself, I realized I was still in the storm. Still in the pain. Still, not healed. My heart was sick. He had not healed me.

Proverbs 13:12 NLT
"Hope deferred makes the heart sick, but a dream
fulfilled is a tree of life."

Get Bitter, or Better

My bitterness not only grew against people, but I also turned against God. But as I pushed Him away from me emotionally, he would always make his way back into my life. My depression and bitterness felt as if I was drowning, trapped in deep waters. The waters were dark, and hope was dim. Life gave me moments of gasping for air before sinking back into the depths.

In seventh grade, I reached a point where I was almost unreachable by friends and family. During this season, my sister was introduced to a new church in town, and we connected with their youth group.

Thankfully, the depths of my darkness were not allowed to go any deeper. The church was Baptist, and they loved me despite my bitter roots. God wanted me to work through my pain and not get lost in it.

In eighth grade, He spoke to me and told me I could continue to be bitter or get better. This year, I chose to love people the best I could. I was still trapped in my disorder, but I could choose to love.

Ephesians 4:31-32 NKJV
"Let all bitterness, wrath, anger, clamor, and evil
speaking be put away from you, with all malice. And be
kind to one another, tenderhearted, forgiving one another,
even as God in Christ forgave you."

10th Grade Year

I wore wigs from 6th grade up until the middle of my soph-

19

omore year in high school. I went through a season of not pulling my hair as much. Underneath my wig, scalp hair began to grow. It was a season to regain some of my sanity, although it was short-lived.

One weekend, my sister had all her friends over from school. They were getting ready for a dance. Hair spray floated in the air as teenage girls were locking in curls. I took off my wig in my room and went down the hallway to the living room to watch a movie. I wasn't going to the dance, so I was ready for a night to stay in. It didn't take long for curious girls who saw me without my wig to pull me into the room. I became an experiment with makeup and hair styling. My hair was about two inches long. And for the first time since my disorder started, I didn't have any bald spots.

As the styling continued, gel, hairspray, and glitter were used excessively. I was a finished product of glittery spiked hair. Surprisingly, all the girls liked it. I received compliments stating that I could get away with having short hair.

I spent the rest of my weekend contemplating whether I should have this as my new hairstyle. When the weekend was coming to a close, I decided to toss my wig and style my hair short. It was my hair, and I finally had something back. Monday morning, I stepped on the school grounds. Walking down the sidewalk, I felt a strength in my heart from God. There was no turning back. I thought, "I'm at my high school. I don't have a wig on. It's happening."

Tenth grade was a season where I could breathe better. It was a season where I could stretch out. But, the season lasted only a short time. My hair grew longer. And the pulling started again. I hid the bald spots the best I could. The episodes of hair-pulling were in full swing again. I had to do life despite spending many hours pulling out my hair. As the days passed, I thought I would stop. Each day, I pulled out my hair, and each day, I was trapped.

Eighteen

Insanity, as defined by Albert Einstein, is doing the same thing over and over again, expecting different results. Though I have never completely cracked, there were moments when I came close. Moments of screaming in my car when I was alone. Moments of crying myself to sleep. Moments, several moments. Several years.

When I was eighteen years old, I was home alone one night. My anxiety was intense; my hair-pulling was out of control. I spent hours pulling out my hair and then skin-picking. I had been seeing a psychiatrist and was prescribed medication that was supposed to lessen my anxiety and depression. While I was wasting hours pulling out my hair, my eyes glanced at this bottle. A thought came to me. It was a demonic thought. I didn't know then.

You should take this bottle of pills. That way people can see the torment you are actually in. No one believes you. People think you are faking this.

I grabbed the bottle. Pressed down on the top with the palm of my hand. The safety lock was released. I poured pills into my hand and began swallowing them. I waited for some time. I didn't know what would happen to me. And what the reaction is for those types of pills. I was alone.

Who would find me if something happened?

I called a man who was an old youth leader from my church. It was late at night, but thankfully, he answered his phone. He was out of town but sent his wife to my house, and she took me to the emergency room. The ER was packed with people waiting. I got a bed right away. The doctor called poison control, and they instructed him to administer charcoal. The cup was black. I held it up to my lips. "I have to drink this?" I asked, confused.

"Yes you do," chimed in a busy nurse. I drank the black chalky drink.

I was in the ER all night. The family did come. But no one was able to see me. Everyone was in the ER lobby. I felt stupid for what I had done. I was hurting myself in a new way. And thoughts of regret flooded my emotions. Not only was I hurting myself, I hurt others now.

I was placed under a 5150 hold. In the state of California, it's a 3-day hold for psychiatric evaluation and protection. In my case, I was under this due to wanting to harm myself. I was transported by ambulance to a psychiatric facility in Riverside County. I was on the gurney in restraints. I needed close supervision being on a 5150 hold.

Two girls were my ambulance crew. They had blue uniform sweaters on. They seemed to have their life together—more than mine. One of them handed my medical paperwork to the staff at the front entrance. I waited on the gurney before they wheeled me back. As I glanced at one of the EMTs, I felt a tug at my heart. I didn't want to be the person I was on this gurney. I wanted to be the girl who was strong next to me, the girl who was helping others. I wanted to be that EMT.

My name was called from a door that opened. They wheeled me on the gurney through the open door. A security guard was waiting for me. The door closed, and I was assisted off the gurney. I had a ribbon on my shirt that wasn't long. It was hanging down close to my chest. The security guard had one crooked eye and one eye that moved. I couldn't tell if he was staring at my chest or not. It made me feel very uncomfortable. He stared for a long time. "We need to cut that ribbon off. No shoe laces or strings of any kind are allowed in here," the security man spoke up. He cut off the ribbon on my shirt.

My shoes and belongings bag were taken. I thought I was going to be moved to another place. Another room. But the door soon closed behind me. The staff member helping me check in walked through another door. A thick glass shield protected this room. It looked like a bulletproof window.

I walked the small hallway to the main lobby, where I was to stay. This facility had all the psychiatric patients stay in one area, and the staff watched them through the thick glass-protected window. I was with the mentally ill! My mind was screaming, *this is not who I am! This is not where I belong!* One of the patients had a helmet on her head. She slammed her head into the walls. The patients were randomly walking around. There were recliner chairs lined up. TVs were on.

I saw a payphone in the middle of the room. I tapped on the glass. A sound beeped, and a nurse spoke through a speaker asking what I needed.

"I want to call my mom," I said.

They arranged for a call. I stood by the phone, and within minutes, I heard it ring. I answered it. My mom was on the phone. Crying, I told her where they had sent me. I was in panic mode at this time. My heart was screaming: *This wasn't me. I'm not crazy.* She got off the phone soon after to complain to the staff. But there wasn't anything my mom could do. I was under a hold. The only way out is for a doctor at that facility to clear me.

"My daughter doesn't belong there. She is afraid. Is there anything you guys can do?"

"Not at this time ma'am. Later tonight, we will medicate her so she will sleep."

When I heard that report, I panicked even more. I saw an open room with 5-8 beds. I would have to sleep in the same room with all the other patients. My mind wandered to that security man who was looking at my chest. *Would he hurt me?* I cried again. With persistence on my part and my mother's, the staff arranged for a doctor to evaluate me later that evening.

A few hours passed. Police brought in a lady in handcuffs.

She had lost her mind. She was kicking and screaming. She didn't respond well to anyone. They walked her over to a white padded room. She was placed in there, and the door was locked. I saw her face in the small glass window as she looked at all of us. She screamed at the top of her lungs and slammed her hands against the door. The medical staff didn't take long to enter the room. About six people were gathering around this woman. They pinned her down on the ground and gave her a shot to calm her. My anxiety was high. *God, please! I don't want to spend the night here!*

Within a couple of hours, things changed. By God's grace, a man came into the room and asked me to sit at one of the tables with him. He was the doctor. He had the power to say what he wanted to do with my life. He mentioned he usually doesn't do this type of evaluation until daytime. But he made an exception. He asked questions. It didn't take him long to conclude I didn't belong there. And he cleared my 5150 hold.

My stepdad picked me up from the psychiatric facility that night. I am thankful I did not have to stay there any longer. Being in a room full of crazy people will make you feel crazy yourself. God gave me a glimpse of what my life could turn into. My perception of my pain needed to change. I couldn't drown myself in self-pity.

When I was nineteen years old, I went into the EMT program. There was a vision of strength I wanted when I saw that ambulance girl. I wanted to help people and not be a lost soul. I could have a downward spiral of bitterness and self-harm, or I can stand up and do something with my life.

Hebrews 12:15 NIV
"See to it that no one falls short of the grace of God and that no bitter root grows up to cause trouble and defile many."

CHAPTER 4- MIRRORS

A thought came to me when I was a young girl. It was the same annoying demonic voice that has haunted me for years with false wisdom.

Look in the mirror and tell yourself you're ugly. So you stop destroying yourself.

I looked at myself in the mirror. I had a bald head with just some patches of hair trying to grow back. I had no eyebrows or eyelashes. "You are ugly, Erin". I spoke over myself. "Look how ugly you are. STOP PULLING YOUR HAIR OUT!" I glanced at myself in disgust.

Unexpected Miracle

One of my biggest mistakes was believing the LIE that I would one day just "grow out" of my disorder. Middle and high school passed, and I was now in college. Long hours of studying for respiratory school became an intense battle for me. My hair-pulling was getting out of control. For the first time since sixth grade, it was getting harder to hide the baldness. I was losing so much hair. And it was getting to the point I needed to wear a wig again.

In desperation, I cried out to God one evening. I prayed for help! I envisioned my prayers reaching past the roof and floating into the sky. The prayers continued the journey, making its way into space. *God, where are you? I know you can hear me. I know you have the power to give me a full head of hair.*

Two weeks later, I was scrolling through YouTube videos. I came across a hair salon in London that specialized in placing an Intra-lace hair system for women who battled hair loss. This particular video was about a teenage girl who battled hair-pulling. The hair gets sown into the natural hair by a netted placement. I was happy to see a hair salon helping people in this way. But I was also discouraged because I could never experience that.

My curiosity took over, and I searched online. At the top of the website was a description of the grand opening of a new salon. When I clicked on the site, I saw that it was in Beverly Hills, California, a two-hour drive from where I lived. A woman named Lucinda Ellery was the owner. After investigating further, I found that models were needed. Ten models were to get the intra-lace hair system in place. Pictures would be taken to show the before-and-after to the public. I filled out the interest form.

Some time passed, and I was in a study group in my class. We were at a coffee shop when I received a call from a Lucinda Ellery employee. He scheduled a free consultation for me. He informed me that not everyone would get picked, but I should still come.

Leading up to the consultation, I decided to do something I had never done before. I fasted—I had no food for two days. My fear of wigs was embedded in my soul, and it hurt my heart to think of wearing one again. I didn't know what else to do. I couldn't drop out of school because of stress. I needed to finish. There was no easing into this fast. The sudden shift to no food took its toll on me. But this was an emergency for me. I needed help. I didn't tell anyone what I was doing. I didn't think I would get the support since I was in school and needed my strength and energy for my studies. I pressed through, barely.

My first consultation day came. The front doors of the salon were closed. I walked through the back door to get in. As I stepped in, the scent of candles filled the room. Stepping into the salon felt so refreshing. It was beautiful in there. There was a woman in a salon chair getting her hair done. Her baldness was showing. They had a protected atmosphere there for women to feel safe. A folded wall stand blocked the front windows. I felt at home in that place. They understood me. The consultation went well. The hairstylist measured my hair loss to determine how much to sow in the intra-lace system. Hopeful, I put my trust in God. I had done all I could by praying and fasting.

The day soon came when I received my follow-up call. Lucinda's son, Chris, was helping build their new location in L.A. "Erin, we have good news! We want to bless you with the hair system," said Chris. I shrieked. This hair system costs thousands of dollars to put on, and God had just blessed it to me for free. The maintenance costs were for me to handle, but the beginning was huge. *Thank you for hearing me God.*

First Intra-lace System

The day I was scheduled to be at the salon, I got help with the drive from my sister and her boyfriend. The appointment was eight hours long. Sitting in that chair was such a blessing. I had never experienced a hair salon like that. The times I went to a hair salon in the past, my bald spots were in view for all to see. I felt embarrassed as people walked by me.

After those embarrassing moments, I took matters into my own hands and did my hair at home. I would bleach and use toner. I would cut my hair as well. Having bald spots on my sides, I usually always had it pulled up in a bun, so my haircuts didn't have to be perfect.

That hair salon made me feel special. I had a tea set and biscuits next to me. With the hair wash, I felt something I hadn't felt in many years. I didn't have to be ashamed of how I looked. I was free to be around people. They didn't care I was half bald. They specialized in it. These were little moments. Moments of feeling cared for. Moments where I could let my protective guard down. Small moments that were making a change in me. It was a glimpse, a breath of fresh air in a dry and weary world.

The hair I did have was pulled through tiny net holes. When there was a small cluster of hair, it was locked in to stay in place. This was a lot of work for the woman who was doing it. Eight hours were wrapping up. I was asked how I wanted my hair styled. The final cut and style were the last steps. I didn't know what to say, so I told her to style how she thought was best. She turned my chair opposite the mirror, and the styling was put to work. The woman who had just worked tireless hours on my hair had a huge smile on her face. This was the most exciting part. With her face glowing, she said, "You are all done."

She slowly rotated my chair to let me face the mirror. I kept my eyes closed until the movement stopped. This was my moment to be put together finally. Excitement was in my heart. God, the miracle worker made a way! I opened my eyes to see the new version of myself. My heart sank. My wounded soul was triggered. I was looking not at my current self, but at the image of a broken schoolgirl. A flashback from the past hit me. It looked like the hairstyle I had from my wigs in middle school. I tried to hold back the tears. It was like a filter. I was looking at myself, but another image was placed over me.

I left there confused. I didn't like my hair. I pretended to sleep in the back seat so I wouldn't have to talk on the drive home. My head hurt from the long hours of tugging at the hair for the placement of the intra-lace system.

I called Lucinda Ellery. She was at the salon. I told her my feelings. She was understanding of what I was saying. She has been in this industry for many years and knew the emotional ups and downs. She told me I would like the hair once I got my first wash. The hair system loosens and flows more easily. They could also thin out some of the hair if I wanted. I had a lot of hair! And I wasn't used to it. I fought the process of wearing a wig. And I didn't want it to look like one. After the first wash, I did have them thin it out.

Once again, I went to school. It was different from my 6th-grade and sophomore years. The hair was nicer. Being in college, people were different. They didn't care. The ones that did notice, complimented me. I was in a new arena and thankful for that. I didn't have to worry about being mistreated. God gave me a full head of hair. It wasn't how I expected it to happen. It was a practical solution. He didn't zap me with his power and poof, hair! A salon that specializes in hair loss blessed me with their work. God used the talents and works of their hands. He moved in favor for me.

My Healing Journey Begins

As he brought me forward in my healing journey, there was a glimpse of what was inside of me. There was a depth to my brokenness that needed healing. His gentle hand was leading me forward. And as the waves crashed over me over the years, there were new waves. But these waves were headed in the opposite direction. What first became a leak of dirty waters out of my soul turned into floodgates. My emotions were unexpected at times. What I said and did was a reaction of my wounded soul. Soul wounds have a response when triggered. Soul wounds can speak. I needed God to speak louder. So many voices, so many noises.

The Holy Spirit spoke: *Your past hurts were not your fault Erin, but it's your responsibility to heal now.*

The Small Victories Add Up

Over the next couple of weeks, I felt a shift in my daily routines. I didn't have the burden of spending time adjusting my hair to hide my bald spots. I could freely walk out of the house. This was something I had lost for many years. I noticed a difference in my shower routines. When I took showers with my bald head, my hair would be wet and weighed down. I felt shame. Every shower I took, I was reminded that I was bald. Emotionally, I would try to block the fact that I was so bald. I felt trapped in this world, and it was my strategy to make it throughout my days. When I had the intra-lace hair system placed, I had a full head of hair. It was a moment in my life to be free. To feel free. I didn't have to fight years trying to get my hair back. It happened in one day.

It was a breath of fresh air before the other moments attacked me again. I needed those moments to regain strength and keep going. I would look in the mirror and see I didn't look bad. I was ok. But I noticed throughout my day my feelings of being ugly and insecure would come back. As strange as it sounds, I forgot what I looked like. My feelings would adjust back to how I felt before the hair. My outside appearance was changing slowly, but my soul was stuck in the past. "Go to the mirror again, but tell yourself you are beautiful this time," spoke the Holy Spirit one evening.

I picked an outfit from my closet, put it on, and walked over to the mirror. Looking at myself was never easy for me. I tried to smile. It wasn't the greatest smile, but I did it. I felt the gentle direction from the Holy Spirit speaking to my heart. *You may be reflecting brokenness right now, but you don't have to stay broken.* I then told myself good things out loud. I told myself I was beautiful. That God loves me. That I am beautiful just the way I am.

Each day, I began taking pictures on my cell phone. God was conditioning my heart to be comfortable with who I was and not to be lost in a false image of worthlessness and insecurity. When my insecurities would come back, I would look at the photo I took for the day to remind my soul I am becoming someone new. My perception needed to change. This disorder was not just an attack on my hair. It was an attack on my identity. It was an attack on who God created me to be. His hand knit me together. God thought of me and then made me.

Psalm 139:13-16 MSG

"Oh yes, you shaped me first inside, then out; you formed me in my mother's womb. I thank you, High God-you're breathtaking! Body and soul, I am marvelously made!

I worship in adoration -what a creation! You know me inside and out, you know every bone in my body; you know exactly how I was made, bit by bit, how I was sculpted from nothing into something. Like an open book, you watched me grow from conception to birth; all the stages of my life were spread out before you, the days of my life all prepared before I'd even lived one day."

Reflections

Mirrors are a reflection of who we are. As we look in the mirror, we see ourselves. God reminded me of this as I was reading His Word one evening.

James 1:23-24 AMPC

"For if anyone only listens to the Word without obeying it and being a doer of it, he is like a man who looks carefully at his [own] natural face in a mirror; for he thoughtfully observes himself, and then goes off and promptly forgets what he was like."

We are to do what He says as we glimpse into His Word. God talks about a reflection we are to look at and study. It's His Word. And when we walk away from it, we do not forget what we look like. We must not forget to do what He says to do. I needed to study God's Word. There was a depth that God was speaking to me. There was a reflection the Lord was inviting me into.

2 Corinthians 3:18 NLT

"So all of us who have had that veil removed can see and reflect the glory of the Lord. And the Lord—who is the Spirit—makes us more and more like him as we are changed into his glorious image."

There was a glory to glory yet to be revealed, a reflection that was supposed to get brighter and brighter. For my reflection to begin to change, my perception needed to change. I needed more of Him, more of His Word.

God showed me that healing comes in time, but it must be done on purpose. I couldn't just simply wait. I needed action. I needed to intentionally pursue Jesus and his purpose for my life. As He led me to the practical step of viewing a photo of me, to remind me of what I looked like, He then taught me the same applies to remembering a Bible verse. I was to pull out the verse like a photo and reflect on and study it. I was to remember the reflection of His mirror, His Word. So I won't forget it.

In the beginning, it was easy for me to forget what He

said. I needed to be deliberate. Worship became a daily thing for me. I was in a season where God's presence overflowed throughout my days. There seemed to be a honeymoon phase of love for one another. I knew God loved me. During this season, I felt His presence all around me. I listened to worship music all day. I would be woken up in the middle of the night with an invitation to spend time with Him. He loved hearing me worship as much as I loved to worship Him back.

The hair-pulling didn't stop. But the hours of being in His presence lessened the episodes. This was the first time I entered His inner courts. There was a depth I was reaching I never had before. I didn't know He was filling me up to overflow for the journey ahead—a path I never expected to walk down. The path that I surrendered to.

CHAPTER 5- SURRENDERING TO A UNIQUE PATH

I was standing outside. I knew the man I was standing with was Jesus, but I couldn't see his face. He gestured with his right hand for me to move forward. I looked down. There was a yellow gravel path under our feet. I started to follow the path with my eyes. I saw it disappear into a dark forest. I look at Jesus with a puzzled face. "You want me to walk through that?" I asked.

He nodded.

I envisioned a large hand picking me up and placing me on the other side of the forest, bypassing the gloomy dark trees. He knew what I was thinking. I could tell he wasn't going to change his mind.

"I don't want to walk through that."

A wind began to blow directly at me. Bible verses started swirling around me like a whirlwind, speaking to me.

"Trust in the Lord with all your heart."
"Though I walk through the valley of the shadow of death, you are

with me. Your rod and staff they comfort me, they lead me to still waters."

My alarm clock began beeping. I woke up.

Moriah Ministry

I got ready and headed out the door. I had an hour's drive to an event with Kim, my friend from Respiratory Therapy school. She invited me to come with her. This ministry was in Orange County, California.

The room we entered was small. There were about 50 people there. The pastor speaking that day was from Africa. Sitting in the chair, I reflected on my prayer from a few months earlier:

You heal me however you want to heal me. I surrender.

The pastor was reading the Bible passage concerning a woman who sought healing from Jesus. She had an issue of bleeding for twelve years.

Mark 5:25-29 NIV

"And a woman was there who had been subject to bleeding for twelve years. She has suffered a great deal under the care of many doctors and had spent all she had, yet instead of getting better she grew worse. When she heard about Jesus, she came up behind him in the crowd and touched his cloak. Because she thought, 'if I just touch his cloak, I will be healed.' Immediately her bleeding stopped and she felt in her body that she was freed from her suffering."

Listening to this story never gets old for me. Consider the courage this woman faced as she went against culture and extended herself to the one who could heal– her weighing the risks. She suffered much. She was alone. I could relate to her. The Bible documents what she thought: "If I just touch his clothes, I will be healed."

I was thinking while the message was being preached. *What if God gave her this thought?* Jesus was walking past her, and there was a window of opportunity.

After the lesson, the African preacher roamed around the room. God's Spirit led him to choose people. This was a healing event. I was there for my own healing. I felt the tangible presence of God filling the atmosphere. The Spirit of Prophecy flowed out of this man. At one point, he brought a person to the center of the room and revealed the hidden secret of suicidal thoughts. This individual was planning on killing himself later that day. God knew of this and interceded. People were falling to the floor.

He prayed over another person. But this time, it was different. Pure hate covered this person's face as the African man was praying. And then it happened. "Come out in the name of Jesus," he commanded. His animated African accent made it sound even better. The person yelled and made other noises before dropping to the floor. This person had a demon. And it was being cast out. This was the first time I had ever seen that in real life. There was a sense of peace in the room. I saw a demon coming out of a person in real time. The Holy Spirit spoke to my heart. *Yes, I still heal today, and yes, demons are still cast out today.*

The pastor pointed his index finger up toward heaven, using animated movements to get his point across. He said, "If the enemy is perceived as more powerful than God, then you are doing deliverances wrong."

He picked a handful of people and the session was wrapping up. I thought to myself, *he's not going to pick me. This is taking too long.* So, I raised my hand.

As he began walking over to me, he began to laugh. Another pastor who was at his side mentioned how I was just like the woman with the issue of blood, desperate to touch

Jesus' clothes. If only they knew the torment, then they would understand. I was screaming on the inside. They motioned for me to walk with them. When I was standing in the middle of the room, I felt all eyes on me.

"How can we pray for you?" the pastor asked.

"I battle pulling out my hair." I said.

They didn't look that concerned. So, I pointed at my head and told them most of my hair was gone. What I had on my head was an intra-lace hair system. (Hair weaved into the little I had left). People gathered around me and started to pray. I was hoping to have a breakthrough like the other people in that room. That there would be a celebration in knowing I AM HEALED.

I began to feel a slight buzzing running through my body, and my legs started to sway. I fell to the floor. I was only down for a little bit and returned to my seat. It didn't feel like anything had changed, just some tingling throughout my body. By this time, the event was over. People were randomly scattered throughout the room, talking and enjoying coffee and snacks. I made my way closer to one of the pastors sitting down. There were a handful in that room. But I felt drawn to ask this one.

"How long does it take for someone to be set free from a tormenting disorder?" I asked.

He looked at me and said, "Usually a handful of our sessions."

Hidden Within

My persistence paid off. Within 20 minutes, the pastor got a team together and brought me to a private room. The pastor who had set up this unplanned meeting was a kind man. He was a tall, older gentleman. As I walked with him, I noticed he had a slight limp. His right side had a noticeable weakness, maybe from a past injury or stroke. I sat on a couch with a small gathering of people staring at me—such love and compassion in their eyes. The pastor with the limp right side, sat in a chair in front of me. "So, how can we pray for you?"

I told them, "I battle a hair-pulling disorder, and I can't stop. I pull out almost all of my hair. I feel tormented. The disorder is called Trichotillomania."

"Ok. I want you to know that every name must bow in Jesus' name. And since we know the name of your disorder, we will command it to be submitted under Jesus," said the pastor.

I closed my eyes. I bowed my head. Finally, I will be free!

The pastor spoke, "I command the spirit of this infirmity, Trichotillomania, to come up front and center in Jesus' name." His voice was authoritative but unusually soft. The commands were repeated a few times.

Nothing happened.

I opened my eyes. The pastor looked at me and said, "Erin, sometimes the enemy hides behind our past sins. Let's have you bring it to God and have Jesus cleanse you with the blood."

By the Holy Spirit's leading, there would be a flash memory from my past. Then, I would confess my sin out loud to everyone in that room. I would ask God's forgiveness and ask Jesus' blood to wash it away. There were moments from my past that were very uncomfortable to share. These life moments included watching pornography at a young age, taking pills at 18 years old, and being sexually active in my teen years and early twenties. Some were moments from my past I had never shared with anyone. Ever.

I soon realized everyone in that room had gone through this process. There was no shame or condemnation. They were encouraging me to keep going. They knew the power of confessing. I realized that the next step in my healing journey was coming out of hiding and confess those festering dark secrets. Two verses kept repeating in my heart as I was going through this process:

1 John 1:9 NIV
"If we confess our sins, he is faithful and just and will forgive us our sins and purify us from all unrighteousness."

James 5:16 NKJV
"Confess your trespasses to one another, and pray for one another, that you may be healed."

He commanded again, "spirit of Trichotillomania, come forward in Jesus' mighty name!"

As he was speaking, I had a vision while my eyes were closed. I saw in my stomach a short ugly creature scrambling through a stack of pictures. It was brown in color, had long arms, and had a basic bodily figure. It was frantic as it was throwing photos everywhere. An understanding in my heart flowed as I saw this vision. It was trying to hide behind my past unconfessed sins. And there wasn't much left. I opened my eyes and told them my vision. Excitement filled the room as the people knew their authority in Christ.

"Let's keep going," stated the pastor.

I confessed anything that flowed into my memory. I repeated the process of asking for God to forgive me and asking for the blood of Jesus to wash me clean. The pastor prayed over me. He believed that the prayer of a righteous person has great power as it is working (James 5:16b).

It was time for the "power encounter" prayer again. I closed my eyes and lowered my head. I surrendered to the process. I sat there relaxed.

"I command the spirit of infirmity to come up front and center in Jesus mighty name," spoke the pastor. "Up, up, now. In Jesus' mighty name. I command you now, no more hiding. I forbid it. Come up! You have nowhere else to hide."

Something strange started to happen to my head as the

pastor was making his commands. It wasn't from me, although it was my body moving. My head began to sway back and forth slowly. It swayed to one side, then would move to the other. The swaying got stronger and stronger, and I thought, *there you are!*

In a soft voice, the pastor told the spirit to leave. My head started to move faster back and forth as if saying no. A laugh came out of me. It was my voice, but not me orchestrating it. The sound was strange. It sounded like a hyena laughing.

The pastor then commanded, "Get out spirit of mockery."

My breathing pattern changed, and I started to breathe hard in and out. The breathing became deeper and more forceful.

"You MUST come out in Jesus' name. You have no more legal right to be there. Out now! Out. Come out."

Then, it stopped.

All of it stopped as if my last breath was the exit point for the dark spirit to leave. It was gone. I opened my eyes. I sat there for a moment, looking at everyone. There was an emotional pull for me to be embarrassed for what had just happened. But it wasn't me! And I was genuinely thankful for it to come out. There were closing discussions about what had happened and how I would move forward.

As drawn out as that process was, our time was up. Everyone surrounded me and placed their hands on me. They prayed for protection over me and God's favor. I thanked everyone for their time. As I was walking out, someone mentioned they had sessions for deliverances, which they called power encounters. I signed up.

I have never been delivered from anything before. *Spirit of mockery?!*

Spirit of Mockery

God chooses the order in which demons are cast out.
Jennifer LeClaire, a popular deliverance minister, explains that God can choose to cast out demons in the order in which they first came in or from last to first. Demons can have layers to them. A mocking spirit can guard and hide the other demonic layers.

The first question to ask oneself if they are dealing with a spirit of mockery is, "Am I in right standing with God?"

A mocking spirit knows what you're hiding. As for me, it was going through my past like a stack of photos, looking for what things to hide behind. Hidden sin and unconfessed sin will keep this demon hiding, operating, and blocking. He is at the guard post, not letting you access the depths of God and breakthrough.

Jennifer LeClaire quotes in one of her teachings about this spirit:

> "Sometimes the mocking spirits will accuse you of things
> you did not do, but usually those would roll off your
>   back. But if you did do it, the demonic networks
>   communicate and mock you to try to derail you."

There were actual whole demonic networks staged against me. And the first layer broke. There's a warfare strategy darkness uses. Hiding is the first layer.

We must confess our sins, and turn away from them.

Sandals Church

I attended a large church in southern California called Sandals Church. A while after attending the healing event from Moriah Ministries, God opened another door. My church offered Christian counseling. This type wasn't the average counseling session. It was more spiritual and deeper. They called them deep healing sessions. The wait to get into these sessions averaged six months. But God made a way. The surrendering to his will continued.

Repenting and Renouncing

It was already dark out. I walked into the door on the backside of the church. This was where the extra offices were. I entered a small room that looked like a pastor's office. This was my first session. It was an introduction to the deep healing sessions.

I was guided to a room where three people were waiting for me. As I sat, I glanced to my left and saw a small table with two bottles of water. Next to the water was a stack of papers stapled together. The session began with prayer. This wasn't a basic prayer some may be used to. This was a prayer taking authority over the room and session. The enemy was commanded not to disrupt or interfere. The Holy Spirit was invited to come and invade that space.

Come, Holy Spirit, come.

After praying, everyone looked up. All three who were leading the session looked at me. We all sat in chairs facing each other. There were two females and one male. They began to advise me on how the first session would go. I was to read the packet that was to my left out loud—all of it. The waters were for me. This was going to take almost two hours.

"So, we want you to read it out loud," said the male. "If you stutter or mispronounce words, we will have you go back and reread it." He smiled.

"Ok", I said.

"Also, sometimes you may not even see a word or sentence. When this happens, it's the enemy blocking you from seeing. So we'll ask you to go back over that too."

Everyone had the same packet to follow along. I began reading the first page. I repented and renounced past sins from me and my ancestors. The pages had depth to it. Every word and sentence was breaking any legal rights that may have happened over my life or from past generations.

Proverbs 28:13 NIV
"Whoever conceals their sins does not prosper, but the one who confesses and renounces them finds mercy."

My eyes landed on the next section. "I repent and renounce any involvement by me or my ancestors in all occult practices. This includes tarot cards, crystals, Ouija boards, horoscopes, fortune telling, magic eight ball, spirit contacts, conjuration, necromancy, Raki and transcendental meditation, seances, sorcery, astor projection, black magic, white magic light as a feather, automatic handwriting, palmistry." I spoke out loud.

As I continued to read, I got to the section on freemasonry. The male helping lead the session had me pause. He sensed something was there, "Did you have any involvement in freemasonry?"

"I never met my dad, but I heard he was into Wicca. He was abusive to my siblings, so he went to jail. I'm not sure about freemasonry."

"Look into that some more. We will seek the Holy Spirit on it too."

The packet indeed was long. I was thankful for the water to press through to the end. The session was done, so the three gathered around me to pray before leaving. They all laid their hands on my shoulders and back. I closed my eyes. I heard their voices praying, but I was suddenly caught up in a vision.

I saw a goat man figure standing up straight like a man; it had large twisted horns. The vision faded to another one, a human figure shining as a bright light. That vision faded to one more. It was a huge eye. This eye looked real. As I stared at this eye in my vision, I pondered how weird it was to stare at something with my eyes closed. I then began to study the eyelashes. The eye covered the whole picture frame of my vision. It was just one big eye. As I continued to look at it, the eye moved to stare at me directly. Fear came over me.

The prayers were still happening, but I interrupted. "I am getting visions while you are praying." I described to them my visions, especially about the eye. And how it scared me. They didn't understand what the visions meant but prayed for protection over my family and me.

I walked to my car and called my friend Kim. (God led this friend to invite me to the Moriah Ministries healing event at the beginning of my healing journey.)

"And then I saw a big eye!" I said over the cell phone.

"You know what the visions mean right Erin?" said Kim.

"No."

"Your first one was some sort of demonic being. The second was Satan. Remember in the Bible, it talks about Satan masquerading as an angel of the light? The last vision is the eye from freemasonry."

2 Corinthians 11:14 NLT
"But I am not surprised! Even Satan disguises himself as an angel of light."

I was shocked. During the session, I recalled how freemasonry was highlighted when I was reading through the packet.

"I can help you, Erin. I have a packet for you to read to break the covenants with freemasonry. It takes about an hour."

I went through the packet of renouncing and repenting of freemasonry in my bloodline. My friend helped me through that process. Having a strong Christian leading me through the prayer is wise.

Proverbs 24:6 NASB
"For by wise guidance you will wage war, and in an abundance of counselors there is victory."

CHAPTER 6- INCEPTION

Movies have been a way of connecting for my daughter and me. We love to snuggle on the couch with popcorn. One of the movies that struck me was "Inception," starring Leonardo DiCaprio. In this movie, a hired team can enter a person's dream world without permission. In the dream, thoughts and ideas can be placed. The team uses this to deceive a person into doing what they want them to do. The greatest deception and the most successful mission result when they can make the person believe the thought came from themselves. Then, the person will not question it or fight against it. The lie can settle and take root.

(Spoiler alert if you haven't watched the movie.) A husband, played by Leonardo DiCaprio, was practicing this dream world with his wife. Unfortunately, they got stuck. He placed a lie in his wife's deepest subconscious. Once they were brought back to the real world, that deep-embedded lie changed her reality. The lie was still inside her. She believed the lie over what she saw and felt and was trapped in its torment. The lie was that her life wasn't real, and she would have to kill herself to wake up from her dream. Tragically, she killed herself, thinking she would then wake up. But, of course, she died.

Watching this movie made me think about the demonic realm. Demon's place lies deep within us, and a series of decisions occur upon that inception. Someone's whole world can shift and change because of a statement or phrase deep within them.

Inception is the beginning. The Holy Spirit can go through our souls and memories and go to the beginning of when that lie took place. Deep healing is searching for the lie, finding it, destroying it, and replacing it with truth. God's truth can replace the lie through a statement, a Bible verse, an image, or a movie-like vision. Healing takes place. There are things we know are there, but also things we never knew were placed. They can be hidden away, like in a locked safe deep within our subconscious.

For almost two decades, I had believed the lie, "*No one understands me.*"

Deep Healing

After a few completed meetings, it was time again for my deep healing session at Sandals Church. I had a good understanding of the flow of the session. The Holy Spirit would lead us. Visions would come to people in the room as we searched deep into my soul, deep into the parts of me that needed healing.

As I took my seat, I was welcomed with warm smiles. Three women were leading this session. They always tried to connect me with the same people, so the sessions flowed more easily.

After praying, one woman began to talk, "Ok, where would you like to begin? We can go as far back as when you were a baby or in your mother's womb."

As she spoke, the Holy Spirit tugged on my heart. He said, *"No, I want you to focus on your sixth-grade year."* I told the girls in the room what I heard the Holy Spirit say.

"So, Erin, tell us about your sixth-grade year." One woman said.

I was 28 years old, sitting in that chair, but the memories were still fresh. The pain was still there. It reminded me that my soul was hurt and needed to be fixed. But I never knew how to do it. So, my 28-year-old self recalled my memories of my sixth-grade year. I told them everything. I shared an image or thought that surfaced until I felt done. The session fell silent. In compassion, one girl had tears running down her cheeks.

One woman broke the silence by saying, "Holy Spirit, bring Erin back to the hard moments so she can walk through them with Jesus."

I closed my eyes. As I sat there, one girl asked me, "Where is Jesus Erin?" I had a vision. My little sixth-grade self, with my awkward itchy wig, was holding Jesus' hand. I was standing on the playground, where all the teasing took place. Kids were running around as if it was a typical day at school. I glanced up at Him. He was tall from my viewpoint, although I could not see His face. In the deep healing session, someone asks, "Ok, where do you want to go with Jesus first?"

"I want to go to the boy who threw the handball at my head," I said.

Our steps began; we walked together across the cement playground. Kids were running around, talking, laughing, and the swings were making shrieking noises. We stopped in front of the wall where kids played handball. The little boy stood before us with the red rubber ball under his arm to keep it in place. While my vision was happening, I heard a woman's voice speaking, "It's time you forgive this boy for what he has done to you." Bible verses are said out loud to validate this vital truth. God calls us to forgive others just as Christ has forgiven us (Ephesians 4:32). God's Word has the highest authority over my feelings and personal thoughts.

"But I feel like I'm losing if I forgive," I said. My eyes were still closed as I was in this vision.

"It's not harming him if you don't forgive. It's harming you."

My vision continued as if I had pressed a play button. Jesus. The boy. I must forgive.

"Say it out loud Erin. You can say it multiple times until you feel a release." One woman said.

I then said aloud, "I choose to forgive the boy with the red ball for... hurting me, embarrassing me, making fun of me. I choose to forgive in the name of Jesus." I choose! It's my choice. I am standing with Jesus. I have the power to forgive because Jesus forgave me. Now, I can use His strength to forgive others. I forgave him. I released him.

"Now Erin, stay in this spot a moment. In the Bible, God talks about not only to forgive people but to ask God to bless them" (Romans 12:14). As she was speaking, in my vision, I turned to look at Jesus. He had a wrapped present in his hands. My sixth-grade self picked up the gift and handed it to the boy.

In the session, I prayed out loud, "Jesus bless this boy wherever he is now. Wherever he is today as a grown man, I pray you will bless him and give him a gift." After praying, I felt a supernatural release. I truly forgave, and I asked God to bless him.

After that, I went with Jesus to other parts of the playground where I was hurt. I repeated the process. It was a beautiful time. God supernaturally healed those broken parts of my soul. The emotional pain from those experiences was replaced with Jesus. I no longer remember the teasing and the hurt as painful memories. My 6th-grade year was replaced by a scene of Jesus and me walking on the playground—me holding his hand, Jesus making things right, Jesus giving me the power to forgive. It's like a movie clip within my soul now. God transformed my brokenness into a beautiful story.

He Bore Our Shame

We made our way to the school bathrooms, where I would hide during lunch and recess breaks. "Where is Jesus in the room?" One of the women in the deep healing session asked. Another vision came. But it wasn't from me. It came from one of the leaders.

She said, "I see an image of you in the bathroom corner on the floor. You are bald. You are curled up in a fetal position, crying." (This was figuratively speaking since I never did that there. But the Holy Spirit was showing my emotional state with images.)

The woman getting the vision continued, "I see Jesus. He is sitting on the floor next to you. He has a loving smile on his face as he looks at you. He is bald too." As she finished that last statement, the Holy Spirit nudged at my heart:

HE BORE OUR SHAME.

I had heard this phrase multiple times, but I felt like I was just gifted with it written on my heart forever. Jesus was bald too. The Bible was made personal to me. I realized God not only saw my shame, but he experienced it. Jesus bore MY shame.

I saw him smiling at my sixth-grade broken self. Love gleamed in his eyes, and his bald head brought understanding. Jesus was also mocked, misunderstood, and hurt by others. He carried pain and shame, but he overcame it. He was a warrior.

The vision faded to another one. Jesus with the crown of thorns being pressed into his scalp. Blood dripped down his face. Jesus knew what shame felt like with my hair-loss disorder. He experienced the pain with me. I battled something I felt alone in. *No one understands you...* But that was a lie! Jesus understands me. In that deep healing session, the Holy Spirit showed me how alive the Bible truly is. It pierces through every moment of my life and has a better story to tell—a story of redemption and restoration.

Isaiah 53:5 (NLT)
"But he was pierced for our rebellion, crushed for our sins. He was beaten so we could be whole. He was whipped so we could be healed."

Jesus didn't take me out of my sixth-grade year—I lived it. And the healing didn't take place until I was an adult. But God saw my past, present, and future with His redemption plan already in place. He saw my brokenness and victory in Christ at the same time. He is God.

Ecclesiastes 3:11 (NLT)
"Yet God has made everything beautiful for its own time. He has planted eternity in the human heart, but even so, people cannot see the whole scope of God's work from beginning to end."

My sixth-grade year was supernaturally healed. I no longer hurt thinking about it. My memories of teasing and humiliation were replaced with new images, with new memories. And these memories were the truth. I chose to forgive those who hurt me. I released them.

God says in his Word that he will never leave us nor forsake us (Hebrews 13:5). My memories of that year altered my perception of reality. The truth was, God never left me. He was right there in the pain with me. But now, I was able to see it. I was not alone in my pain. God understood me. God saw me. He was always by my side.

We looked at my sixth-grade year through God's eyes. I

walked those school grounds with Jesus. We used His Word as a weapon against darkness. We tackled the lie that caused me to be isolated and alone.

There was a photo album I would look at from my past. I always cried as I looked through those pictures throughout the years. It hurt me. The pain of those memories was still in my soul– being alone, being teased.

I was home one evening, and the Holy Spirit nudged at my heart to look through the photo album. I sat on my couch and began to flip through the pages. I saw myself. The one I always saw as ugly and alone. But as I glanced at the photos this time, I noticed I didn't cry. The emotional pain was gone. God healed those moments. He replaced those memories with better ones.

Lies

The Holy Spirit reminded me of another lie that took root in my heart. I was a child when I started to do some deep thinking. I thought about my conception. My parents conceived me before they were married. My mom would always tell me I was her surprise. But as I pondered this, a thought came to my mind: *You are a mistake.* I had to tackle this lie with God's truth. I had believed this for many years.

Other phrases and images would be highlighted to me, and I would replace those lies with God's truth. Some lies took time to overcome. The deep healing sessions made it easy to flow in the supernatural, but I found it took more work when I was alone. I know now that God was training me. I needed to be stronger in Him, to bring His presence and power wherever I was.

Truth is what sets us free. God has a truth to replace all demonic lies. The Holy Spirit can return to the beginning when that lie took root (inception) and remove it from our souls. But… In His choosing. His timing. His ways.

Life is a journey. It is a path we walk down. God will give us practical steps to move forward. Listen to those simple ideas. Then, be open to the more radical things. Surrender your entire life to Jesus. He will heal you piece by piece. Listen to what he says, and then do it.

CHAPTER 7- THINGS THAT BLOCK HEALING

Blurred Face

"Okay, Erin. I want you to close your eyes and ask the Holy Spirit to show you Jesus' face," said one of the women in the deep healing session. I closed my eyes. They prayed out loud for God to reveal Jesus to me. I got a vision. I could tell it was a vision of a man, but it was blurred. I could not see him clearly. I opened my eyes and told the three women in the room that Jesus' face was blurred.

"Holy Spirit, reveal to Erin why she can't see Jesus' face clearly."

I then heard one word. *PRIDE.*

I spoke out loud what I heard God say. They all looked at me, waiting for me to talk more. I waited a moment to understand what I was supposed to do next. Then, words began to spill out from my heart– words that I didn't know were inside of me so strongly. "I didn't deserve this. I was just a child. I've been through so much pain and heartache. Why didn't God let me have a normal childhood? It's not fair I had a hair-pulling disorder." I cried.

"Holy Spirit, show her what she did deserve," one of the women spoke.

I saw Jesus on the cross, his head tilted low towards the ground, and his body covered with old and new blood. As I soaked in this vision, the Holy Spirit spoke to my heart: *"That's what you deserved, Erin."* I couldn't see Jesus clearly, and the reason was pride. Suffering causes our emotions to do some crazy things, and this type of pride was not on my radar. I did not understand how this could be in the same category.

My own words echoed back at me: *I didn't deserve this.* God was showing me what I deserved. And it was on that cross.

You deserved much, much worse.

I began to understand that God would not adjust to my small thinking. I had to mature into His. God didn't soothe me and give me all the answers. He didn't explain why it happened to me. The Bible says that God resists the proud but gives grace to the humble (James 4:6). I needed God's grace. I didn't know this was blocking me from moving forward, from seeing Jesus clearly.

Erin, you deserved much, much worse.

That's Not Jesus

In my vision, I was at the top of the stairs, reliving the season of my life when my mom was married to my stepdad. The top of the stairs led to their closed bedroom door. My stepdad had a loud voice, so their conversations were easy to hear sitting at the top of the steps. It was here that I would listen to him call me the "B" curse word, talk poorly about me to my mom, and say whatever was on his mind. It hurt to hear him talk about me like that. I was a good kid, but having a blended family was difficult. How he handled the home made it more complicated.

I recalled those memories in my deep healing session. One of the women asked, "Where is Jesus in this part of your life, Erin?" I see Jesus appearing at the top of the staircase with me. He looks angry. His hand reaches for my chin and squeezes it. His facial expression refigured to pure hate.

"That's NOT Jesus," one of the women said defensively. They all took authority over that vision and commanded that demonic spirit to leave. It was during this time God showed me how father wounds from my stepdad distorted my view of Jesus. A part of my soul saw Jesus as angry and disappointed with me. In this vision, Jesus hated me. But that wasn't Jesus! A spirit had made its home in my hurtful memories of a broken home.

We Must Forgive

My real dad was absent. I don't remember him. My mom separated from him when I was a young toddler. My memories of him are none. There's a depth of healing needed for my biological dad, which I will discuss later. But healing for my stepdad started in that deep healing session. I had to continue this one alone over the next few months.

My stepdad was the only man in my life. He dated my mother for seven years and was married for seven years, so he was present for fourteen years. And yet, we never had much of a relationship. He would tell me he loved me, but the top of the staircase voiced a different opinion. The longer my mom stayed with him, the more complex the homelife became.

There was a lot to forgive and release. It was all emotional, nothing physical. Out of respect for him, I will not share. My intention in this book is not to shame anyone who has hurt me but to show you the process God led me through. I have forgiven them all.

Unforgiveness blocks healing.

Charles Kraft is a well-known deliverance minister. His focus has been on helping people through inner healing and deliverance. In his teachings, he describes demons like rats. Rats are attracted to garbage. The idea is to remove the garbage first, then the rats. If you kick the rats out with the garbage still there, the rats will return. The same concept applies to casting out demons. It's good to get rid of the garbage in our lives and our souls—the things that led them to us in the first place.

I needed to forgive my stepdad.

In this season, the Holy Spirit gave me a catchy phrase: *"Remember the good over the bad; then you will never be sad."* I would exercise forgiveness at home. I would write down all he did that hurt me, then pray out loud, "I choose to forgive... " I would say the hurts, then repeat it until I felt released.

Forgiveness is a choice. God calls us to forgive. I've already gone through the process in my deep healing sessions from sixth grade. But I had more unforgiveness in my heart. Parents are a huge one to forgive. Unforgiveness can block us from moving forward in our walk with Christ.

God instructs us to honor our father and mother so that all will be well (Exodus 20:12). Honoring your parents does not necessarily mean that they deserve it. You are honoring the title they carry over you—Mom and Dad. You're honoring them as people.

Remember the good over the bad; then you will never be sad.

I recalled the memories of my stepdad attending my tennis games with a video camera. He would smile and watch me play tennis matches. He would always call me by my nickname. Anytime I had my guard down, he would try to stick his finger in my ear to be funny. He paid for my college tuition for the EMT program. When I got my driver's license at sixteen, he gave me his car. He had it detailed and auto parts checked. He said he was proud of me the day he handed over the keys.

I needed to practice this same concept with others who had hurt me throughout the years. *Choose to forgive.*

I went to one particular family member to try to resolve the past. This person hurt me, and I wanted to tell her I forgave her. But the conversation blew back at me. We ended up arguing, and she ignored me for two weeks. God showed me that some people can only be forgiven in private. Reconciliation involves two people. But forgiveness can just be one.

For this particular person, this process took months. When a memory would pop up in my mind during the day, I would say aloud, "I choose to forgive…" and forgive that event. I noticed a current situation would arise, and I needed to forgive her again. She would hurt me, and then I would repeat the steps to forgiveness.

Remember the good over the bad; then you will never be sad.

Remembering a person for the good and choosing to forget the bad is Jesus' superpower– a power that has been made available to us. There's power in forgiving others. It takes strength and courage to do it. I never was a forgiving person. Starting at such a young age, I would hold onto the hurts. I would place a protective wall around myself that wouldn't allow people into my life once they hurt me. God showed me that if I am close to a person in any type of relationship—a friendship, a coworker, a family member— once I am around them long enough, eventually they will hurt me, or I will hurt them.

People make mistakes.

But… I make mistakes too.

The greater the hurt, the greater God can work.

Surrendering my hurts to the Lord changed my heart. I was able to heal.

Kingdom Standards

A Christian is held to a higher standard of forgiveness. Jesus forgave all our sins when we asked him to. He is a forgiving God.

A parable in the Bible, Matthew 18:21-35, describes the kingdom of heaven like a certain king who forgave a servant from a lot of debt owed. This same servant (upon being released from his debt) found someone who owed him much less. And he threatened him to pay back. The king in the parable found out and said, "'You wicked servant! I forgave you all that debt because you begged me. Should you not also have had compassion on your fellow servant, just as I had pity on you?' And his master was angry, and delivered him to the torturers until he should pay all that was due to him," Matthew 18:32-35 NKJV.

This parable contains an unpopular message. There are two parts to it. The first is that God holds forgiveness to a high standard in the kingdom of God because of all that he has forgiven. We should be like God, have compassion, and forgive others.

When the temptation comes to harbor unforgiveness in my heart, I measure what that person did against all my sins. I envision my past, present, and future sins combined. Then I ponder: *Does what they did to hurt me add up to all my sins on this earth that Jesus has forgiven?*

The second important part of this parable is that the unforgiving servant is sent to the torturers until he pays all that is due. Unforgiveness can put a person in a spiritual prison. And the torturers are demons.

Jesus ended this parable by saying, "So My heavenly Father also will do to you if each of you, from his heart, does not forgive his brother his trespasses" Matthew 18:35.

A good Bible verse to know is James 4:7: "Resist the devil, and he will flee from you." There are many ways to get rid of demons in our lives. Casting them out is good. But, in addition, if we read the Bible and obey God, demons must go too! Some go when we practice the Word of God and resist them continually.

For those people who hurt us too deeply, a good practice is to release the injustices to God. When we practice forgiveness, we ask God to take care of it. God is the rightful judge. We can ask God to put it in His books for judgment day.

Ecclesiastes 3:17 NKJV, "I said in my heart, 'God shall judge the righteous and the wicked, for there is a time there for every purpose and for every work.'"

Acts 17:31 NKJV, "He has appointed a day on which He will judge the world in righteousness by the Man whom He has ordained. He has given assurance of this to all by raising Him from the dead."

God sits on his heavenly throne. We can release our injustices and wrongs to Him. Forgiving others is freedom. This lifestyle is the way God intended it to be. This is Kingdom living.

CHAPTER 8- SPIRIT AND TRUTH

Proverbs 3:5-6 NIV
"Trust in the Lord with all your heart and lean not on
your own understanding; in all your ways submit to him,
and he will make your paths straight."

20/20 Vision

We had a guest speaker at my church. He was from Hawaii.
I will never forget his teaching. It was simple, but the
simplicity made it impactful. He had been a pastor for over
thirty years. In his message, he preached the importance of
reading God's Word. The theme of his message was that we
should never feel like we have outgrown reading God's
Word. The lesson included a simple strategy I still use when
I feel stuck. It was called the 20/20 vision. Every day,
preferably at the beginning of the day, read the Bible for 20
minutes straight without interruptions. Then, for 20 minutes,
reflect on what was read and journalize.

I began to practice this. The pastor taught that consistency in spending time with God was necessary. This sermon started my in-depth study of God's Word. There were sessions that lasted longer than this forty-minute time frame. But the daily habit of coming to the Lord for a Word every day shifted things in the supernatural.

The Bible is alive. It speaks. Spiritual warfare would take place. As I attempted to read God's Word more consistently, my hair-pulling would happen alongside it. There was a war to keep me from reading His word, and I knew it was there. Tiny strands of hair would be trapped in the pages of my Bible, and I would find them later when I went back to read more.

What would take people certain amounts of time to finish books in the Bible probably took me two to three times longer. But by God's grace, I read through the whole Bible. After reading through the entire book, God spoke to me and told me, "Now read through it all again."

The second time around, it was faster. The third time around, reading from cover to cover, God repeated, "Now read through the whole Bible again." He was having me sit in front of a reflection, like a person standing in front of a mirror, studying what they look like. He was showing me His Word, His promises, and His character. He was teaching me warfare. Scripture is used to dismantle what darkness has built up. Reading the Bible and having a relationship with God are equally important.

John 4:23-24 ESV

"But the hour is coming, and is now here, when the true worshipers will worship the Father in spirit and truth, for the Father is seeking such people to worship him. God is spirit, and those who worship him must worship in spirit and truth."

The Holy Spirit was ministering to my heart. *The super-*

natural and the Word of God go together. When I began my journey of reading God's word with stamina, a flow began to take place. He was speaking to me through the verses, and the verses seemed to pop out at me.

Sandals Deep Healing sessions intentionally had me declare God's promises over my life. I was assigned homework to study the promises God made to me in his Word.

I am created in the image of God. Genesis 1:27 ESV, "So God created man in his own image, in the image of God he created him; male and female he created them."

I am thought of by God. Psalm 139:17 NASB, "How precious also are Your thoughts for me, God! How vast is the sum of them!"

God has good things stored up for me. Psalm 84:11b NLT, "The Lord will withhold no good thing from those who do what is right."

God loved me first, so now I can love others. John 13:34 NKJV, "A new commandment I give to you, that you love one another; as I have loved you, that you also love one another."

With the breakthroughs I received in Deep Healing and Moriah Ministries, I would assume that my hair-pulling would lessen. But it began to intensify in my life. I had more anxiety. There seemed to be a weight on me that was hard to shake off.

There was a moment when I had a meltdown at home. I felt depressed and wondered if I was doing something wrong. The Holy Spirit told me, "Keep going, don't give up." I could almost hear Him smile as He spoke those words to me.

Am I doing the right thing? Why is it so hard then?

Tower of Faces

Reading God's Word continued. God was building a foundation in my life. I was in a new season of driving my daughter to school and working full-time as a Respiratory Therapist. School lines were a pain. The line of cars waiting for pickup would expand almost half a mile, so I needed to be there early for pickups.

I was in the car line one day. I began scrolling through YouTube videos and found a teaching on "How to Pray in Tongues" by Mark Virkler.

Mark Virkler is a pastor who had an old video series where he taught the basics of praying in tongues. He taught that it's important to know what God says about tongues and understand God's character when we ask for these things.

Matthew 7:9-11 NIV
"Which of you, if your son asks for bread, will give him a stone? Or if he asks for a fish, will give him a snake? If you, then, though you are evil, know how to give good gifts to your children, how much more will your Father in heaven give good gifts to those who ask him!"

While in the car, I got a flashback memory from my past. Bible studies were held at my apartment complex by a man who later was found to be a false prophet. I was a child, and I didn't know. He had laid hands on me to impart the gift of praying in tongues. The Holy Spirit spoke as I recalled this memory: *Pray against what he prayed over you. He blocked this gift.*

In faith, I prayed out loud against what this man prayed over me. I pleaded for the blood of Jesus to wash it away. I rebuked and renounced any involvement with this man. And in my case, all have been done unbeknown to me.

The next day, I was in the car line again, and God had me listen to more teachings from that same series. Mark taught that I was to receive the gift of tongues in faith, just as I received the gift of salvation in faith. I was to know in my heart that if I placed my focus on Jesus and believed that if I asked for the gift of tongues, he would not give me a snake.

There was an activation moment. The teaching detailed the specifics. The sound comes out of our vocal cords, and we had to mutter to get it to start flowing. God was not going to take our tongue and move it.

I started rolling out random "ba, ba, bas" and other silly sounds. I was in the car by myself, so there was no one to judge me. I envisioned a pool of crystal blue water in my stomach. This water began to turn and move. A river began to flow upward, starting from my stomach, passing through my throat, and upwards out of my mouth. And then it happened... tongues began to bubble out of me. I was speaking in tongues. As I was speaking in tongues, the Holy Spirit said to me, "*You already had this gift; it was just blocked.*"

I didn't need anyone else to lay hands on me for this particular gift. I was imparted the gift of tongues. I just didn't know I had it. And I didn't know how to start.

I headed home to take a quick nap before work. I put on a movie for my daughter to watch. As I shut the door to my bedroom, I got into bed. I wanted to pray in tongues more. I was excited about this breakthrough. I had the gift of tongues. God's gifts are irrevocable, Romans 11:29. I will always have this weapon now when praying.

In faith, I uttered noise out of my mouth, and tongues began to flow out of me again. It sounded like a precise language. There was no doubt I had it.

I prayed lying down for about 10-15 minutes. Then, there was a shift in my tongues. My prayer became more authoritative and powerful. My stomach began to tighten. It kept getting tighter and tighter. Then a word flowed out of me in English, "Break, break, break." Even though I said it, those words didn't come from my mind. Those words came from my spirit.

Tongues flowed more, and again, I said in English, "Break, break, break." Then, my stomach softened. My body lay again gently on the bed. I realized I had just been delivered from something. This process happened three times. Tongues would flow, and I would pray out loud in English for it to break off of me.

After the third breakthrough, I got a vision of a tall building. The structure looked to be ten to fifteen stories high. In this building, there were multiple windows. In each window, I saw the face of a demon. My vision zoomed in, and I looked closer as I saw the faces. Each one looked different. After seeing this large building, I heard the Holy Spirit say, "*Now REST.*" I took that invitation gladly. I closed my eyes and slept before work that evening.

I didn't understand what that vision meant until later. God revealed to me there were more demons to expel and to fight off. He knew the journey I was on and that it was not the time to try to fight off everything before work.

Speaking in tongues was a huge breakthrough in my life. It was a weapon of prayer used against the darkness. I didn't know what I was praying. But, there was a trust I developed with God. If he gave me this gift, I knew I could trust the flow of praying in tongues. My spirit, paired up with the Holy Spirit, and went to war with three demonic spirits that day. It felt like the Holy Spirit stretched with his arms and legs in my body and said, "Get out of here; this space is mine!"

Oh sleeper, It's Time to Wake Up

The Word of God and the supernatural go together. God taught me that if I read His Word, I should believe what I am reading. Praying in tongues is a spiritual gift imparted by the Holy Spirit—and what a precious gift it is. If the Bible says it, it's also important to be open to receiving it.

The Bible speaks about believers who are asleep and dead in faith. Those asleep have not been awakened to the spiritual realm and walk blindly throughout their days. Connecting with the Holy Spirit is essential to help you understand why the spiritual realm is absent from your life. There could be blockages. The supernatural does not have to be a scary thing to experience. Hebrews 5:14 AMP says, "But solid food is for the [spiritually] mature, whose senses are trained by practice to distinguish between what is morally good and what is evil." For those who are weak in faith, anything supernatural can be viewed as evil and dismissed.

Over the years, I learned that not everyone will celebrate my deliverance breakthroughs and supernatural encounters. Many have misunderstood me and even become fearful about the stories I shared. It took wisdom to begin filtering the depth of my conversations with people. Not everyone is ready to embark on this wild journey or to hear that demons are fighting against them.

We are in the end times, and God is purifying His church. Daniel 12:10 NIV, "Many will be purified, made spotless and refined, but the wicked will continue to be wicked. None of the wicked will understand, but those who are wise will understand."

If God leads you down this path of inner healing and deliverance, you cannot stop. You must complete the journey. Otherwise, you may be left in a dark forest and can be overtaken. Keep walking, keep moving forward. And don't look back! Awake, oh sleepers, it's time to wake up and fight. It's time to become a pure bride awaiting Jesus' return.

CHAPTER 9- THE WAR WITHIN

My words echoed back at me one evening as I cried out to the Lord, "Why does my life contradict your Word?!"

God promised me good things in life. God promised that I would have hope and a future– that healing was available for me. But I was struggling daily. My body was doing things I hated. My life had glimpses of breakthroughs, but I still felt cursed. *"Erin, you have robbers in your house,"* spoke the Holy Spirit.

I remembered the spirit of mockery that was cast out at Moriah Ministries. The three demonic spirits that were cast out of me during my first night praying in tongues. I came out of the prison of unforgiveness, and those tormenting demons had to flee.

There's more?

My vision of the tower of faces flashed before my spiritual eyes— the tall building of demonic faces.

Yes, there's more.

Temple of God

The Bible reveals that we are the temple of God.

1 Corinthians 3:16-17 NKJV

"Do you not know *that* you are the temple of God and that
the Spirit of God dwells in you? If anyone defiles the
temple of God, God will destroy him. For the temple of
God is holy, which *temple* you are." Emphasis added.

The Bible describes an actual temple that was built. God
instructed his people to build this temple, which had an outer
court, an inner court, and the holy of holies. A priest could
only enter the holy of holies once a year. God's power and
holiness dwelled there. The priest spoke to God openly, in
fear and trembling. We as believers, have layers just like the
Old Testament temple had layers. If God reveals in his Word
that we are like the temple, we can understand how this
temple looks and operates.

Ezekiel chapter 8 was highlighted to me as I went into a
deeper understanding of this concept. Israel, God's chosen
people, were committing sins and worshiping false idols.
God showed Ezekiel what was happening to his temple.

Ezekiel 8:7-10 NKJV

"So he brought me to the door of the court; and when I
looked, there was a hole in the wall. Then He said to me,
'Son of man, dig into the wall,' and when I dug into the
wall, there was a door. And He said to me, 'Go in, and see
the wicked abominations which they are doing there.' So I
went in and saw, and there- every sort of creeping thing,
abominable beasts, and all the idols of the house of Israel,
portrayed all around on the walls."

God's people had corrupted the temple, and God was not

pleased with it. Beasts and idols were engraved on the walls. Jeremiah, the prophet, was an annoying voice to the people of God. He was sent to tell them they would be destroyed if they did not repent of their sins and turn back to the Lord. But they didn't listen to him.

But we are delivered to do these things, was one verse that jumped out at me as I read the Bible one morning (Jeremiah 7:10). God responded, "Has this house, which is called by My name, become a den of thieves in your eyes? Behold, I, even I, have seen it." (Jeremiah 7:11).

God's people still believe that lie to this day. I have been raised to believe it myself. That our salvation gives us the freedom to sin. But it does not.

Matthew 21:13 NKJV
"It is written 'My house shall be called a house of prayer,' but you have made it a 'den of thieves.'"

When we continue to participate in doing these things, our temples can become corrupted, and creatures (demons) can make their homes inside of us.

Ezekiel 7:22 NKJV
"I will turn My face from them, and they will defile My secret place; for robbers shall enter it and defile it."

As a believer, the holy of holies is untouched. This is where the Holy Spirit dwells inside of us. We can already have these things in our temple after accepting Jesus in our hearts. Then, we go on a journey of purifying our temples, a process of sanctification. Or we can bring them in after being saved.

Holding capacity

So, how many demons can a person have? If we look at the story in Mark 5:1-20, Jesus encounters a demon-possessed man who has been living in the tombs. This man had a legion of demons.

Mark 5:8-9 NKJV

"'Come out of the man, unclean spirit!' Then He asked him, 'What is your name?' And he answered, saying, 'My name is Legion; for we are many.'"

The ancient Roman army could have a unit of 3,000-6,000 men for a legion. Other sources have different numbers. Legion is a word used to describe an army, large group of soldiers, or military organization. Jesus asked this specific question for a reason. He revealed not only the large number of demons a person could carry but also that the demons acted as a military unit against the person from within.

This reminded me of the first demon that was cast out of me. The spirit of mockery was at the top. He blocked access to the others. He was one of the weaker ones. There was a military structure in place within me.

A person's capacity is much bigger than our minds can comprehend. We can carry the spirit of God deeper within us and demons in our outer courts. The temple was set up so that the spirit of God could dwell there. Believers argue that a Christian cannot have a demon. But God reveals to us in his Word that if his temple, which housed His Spirit, could be defiled, so could his believers.

The War Within

This military structure is not only to steal God's purpose for a person's life but also to prevent them from accessing the

holy of holies. There's an open portal of heaven within us—
a depth of power, glory, and unlimited access to God. Jesus
was able to cast out thousands of demons in a moment. How
was he able to do this!? His temple was pure. It was clean.
There was NOT one demon inside of him. Not one idol was
engraved on his wall.

Luke 4:34 NASB
"Leave us alone! What business do You have with us, Jesus
of Nazareth?"

I could almost hear the demons shrieking as they said this
to Jesus. Their frustration was that he had nothing in
common with them. He was holy. The power Jesus carried
was amazing.

God wants his people to carry His presence and anointing
in greater measures. God wants his people to purify their
temples and walk in power and authority. God desires us to
do greater works than Jesus did on earth! (John 14:12). Life
is a journey, and purifying our temples takes time.

My inner healing and deliverance journey has been a
decade in the making. There have been some dry seasons and
others that explode with movement. I did not choose this
path; God chose it for me. But every day, as I surrender my
life to Jesus, I allow him to lead my days. My journey is still
happening.

In the rest of this chapter, I will share some stories of me
being delivered from demons. Demons are not a highlight of
our walk with the Lord. But encountering, resisting, and
casting them out is part of a Christian journey. These are not
written in chronological order.

Billy Burke Conference

I was at a two-day healing conference. The moment the

pianist opened the event with piano music, the power of God rested in that place. Billy Burke walked around the room to uplift people's faith. He spoke about God's will for healing and that it was available for all of God's children. Billy prayed over me, praying for healing over my body. My thoughts were on my hair-pulling disorder. *Oh Lord, please! I'm tired of this. Please heal me!*

When I left that conference that evening, I felt unchanged. I began walking to my truck and started to weep. My crying intensified. When I sat in my truck, I cried more. Driving home, the tears kept flowing. My watery eyes made it hard to see the lines on the freeway.

I played worship music loudly in my truck. My prayers turned to tongues. As I was praying in tongues, I felt the war within me, and my tongues got louder and louder. A glaze went over my eyes as I was driving. The spiritual atmosphere changed. In English, something shrieked out of my voice, but I knew it wasn't me. It shouted, "No Lord!!!"

The moment that happened, my crying stopped, my breathing pattern began to regulate, and my eyes became clearer.

I knew something had happened, but I didn't understand at the time. Later, in my quiet time with the Lord, he revealed that the spirit of sadness had been cast out of me while I was driving. I was delivered from a demon on the freeway. I don't suggest that as a deliverance spot to practice. But that is just how it happened.

Dream- Spirit Guide

I dreamt I visited John and Lisa Bevere's home. I was in a room full of people. They were all gathered together with their eyes closed, praying in tongues. I was standing in front of these people. In my dream, I had a revelation that I spoke out loud. I said, "I think my dad assigned me a spirit guide."

When I said that in my dream, I collapsed to the ground and shook as if I was having a seizure; they all prayed for me.

I was delivered from a demon in a dream.

My biological dad was known to practice Wicca and other witchcraft practices. I never met my dad, but the Holy Spirit can reveal things that have been hidden. I believe this was the annoying demonic voice that led me astray for many years growing up. The Holy Spirit replaced my spirit guide, pushing that voice aside, but I still needed deliverance.

Moriah Ministries

I was in a session at Moriah Ministries. Their ministry focuses on delivering people from demonic spirits and equipping them with the power of God. They were working on casting out a constricting spirit—one that would, at times, make it hard for me to function and breathe freely. As they were commanding it to come out, I felt a snake form wrapped around me. The snake was so large it covered my entire body. As they would command it to leave, the grip got tighter. It was slowly making its way up my body and reached my neck. It began to tighten around my neck and hyperextend it.

I remember a time I was trapped in anxiety and called a friend for help. Walking up her driveway to her home, I felt something wrapped around me. This feeling of restrainment and an invisible tightness wrapped around my body often happened over the years. This kind of spirit is called a python spirit.

Dream- Spirit of Heaviness

I dreamt that Jennifer Eivaz (a prophet) visited my home. I was telling her that I needed deliverance from demons. She commanded those demons to come out, although nothing happened. I asked her to spend the night in the room down the hall. In the middle of the night, I woke up in my dream, and I saw demons walking around my bedroom. I yelled for her to wake up, and when she walked in, she commanded the spirit of heaviness to leave. She told me there were three of them.

Family Deliverance

I was on a long fast. I went to an event with my sister and daughter. At the end of the teaching, there was an open invitation for prayer and deliverance. After a couple of people went forward, I felt my heart pounding. There was a push from God to go forward. As I walked up and stood at the front, I saw my daughter walking up too. She felt the same push from God.

I shared my story about my hair-pulling. The woman doing the deliverance prayed for me. There was a great battle within me. As she commanded the spirit out, my head tilted low and shook as if to say, "No." The commands continued, and my body shook until I fell to the floor. And a loud shriek came out of me—I was delivered. My daughter was next.

A familiar spirit was on me and being passed down to my daughter. We were delivered that evening. However, I don't think this was the spirit that caused the hair-pulling. (God chose what he wanted out next.)

Split In Two

I set up a private meeting with a friend from my church. I was battling sexual thoughts that I was having a hard time breaking. It was drawing me to the wrong person. And although I didn't act on them, my thought life was flooded with sexual scenes. As we sat at her kitchen table, she said God told her three things to focus on for that day. He wanted us to focus on the spirit of rejection, the spirit of fear, and the spirit of trauma.

She had me repent and renounce from a few pages she printed out. She prayed over me and anointed my head with oil to break the yoke. Then, she started her deliverance session. She used a technique with me, breathing out hard. It is an exit point for the demonic spirit to leave. A couple of times, she had me stand by her door (with the door open) and have me breathe it out. She saw snakes leave, big ones and a ton of small ones. Alligators also left. This was mixed in with the spirit of rejection and the spirit of fear.

Next was the spirit of trauma. This one was surprising for me to hear since I never had a traumatic event. But there is an area of my life I don't remember. My mom left my dad when I was a toddler, around 1 ½ years old. My dad went to jail for abusing my half-siblings. Even though I don't remember, something may have happened to me while living in that home environment—something stored in my soul.

I got a disturbing vision of the spirit of trauma. It was a body that was naked and had its arms and legs stretched out to the sides. A straight line was placed down the middle. There was a circle in the middle with a demonic symbol. The vision looked like an old photo with spots of blood on it. I asked the Holy Spirit what I was seeing. I heard the words for this vision: Split in two.

This has to do with hidden trauma in my life, something that the Holy Spirit has not yet revealed fully. But I have eyes to see it is there, and I have his grace and power to overcome.

Cleansing the Temples

Throughout my healing journey, God will sometimes reveal what has happened. Other times, it's a journey of revelation over time. God engraved in my heart at the beginning of my walk with him:

Proverbs 3:5-6 NKJV
"Trust in the LORD with all your heart, and lean not on your own understanding; in all your ways acknowledge Him, and He shall direct your paths."

He was more concerned about the condition of my soul than my appearance. He was more concerned about the demons that were still housed in the outer courts of my temple.

God desires for us to clean up our souls and clear the temples. God's will for his people is for them to walk in power and authority and not be a holding place for demons to live.

God saw a deeper problem than just the hair-pulling disorder itself. There was a whole network of demons staged against me. It is God's will to heal us. But he does not want to heal one problem itself. He wants to heal the root causes. He desires to heal every part of us. He desires for us to become whole.

Chapter 10- FRAGMENTED SOUL

1 Thessalonians 5:23 MSG
"May God himself, the God who makes everything holy
and whole, make you holy and whole, put you together -
spirit, soul, and body- and keep you fit for the coming of
our Master, Jesus Christ."

The strategy for my deep healing sessions was slow-paced. The Moriah Ministry was faster and more direct, primarily focused on casting out demons. Sandals Church was longer, and I was tired of the same drawn-out process. But as I look back now, I am so thankful it happened!! And I wish I had been patient for more of it. The impact was huge.

A portion of deep healing sessions focused on my fragmented soul. Over the years of teasing and struggling with my disorder, it left my soul broken. It was like shattered glass. Fragments left everywhere.

Each wave of hardship that hit me left a broken piece. Deep healing focuses on picking up that fragmented soul part, looking at it, and allowing God to heal it. Then, God would fuse it back to my growing, maturing soul. This was not my favorite part of the inner healing. There were so many pieces. I kept thinking, *there's more?!* But I am grateful for what the Holy Spirit was doing in me. He showed me a blueprint of what he does to a person's soul.

Piece by piece.

With a fragmented soul, that soul part does not mature and grow with the rest of the body. It stays stuck in the moment of that person's age when the incident took place. It stays stuck in the painful event. Worldly doctors and psychologists call this the inner child within us. Psychologist Carl Jung has backed this up by teaching it in his studies. Throughout his career, he found that a person's inner child is a part of the subconscious mind and the driving force behind many of his/her emotions and gut reactions.

When we go through life, our inner child (fragmented soul part) can get triggered by something that reminds us of that past hurt where the soul part got stuck. This can cause us to partner with the soul part in its character and manner and react immaturely. Have you ever argued with someone who may have been an adult, but for a moment, you felt like you were talking to a 16-year-old? That person's soul part reacted to the pressure. And you probably were talking to a 16-year-old. God was showing me the depth of this.

Middle school was a huge highlight in healing my fragmented soul parts. The Holy Spirit would bring up a past moment; we would work through it together in the session. Then, I would ask Jesus where he was in this part of my life. I would surrender that brokenness to Jesus. The Holy Spirit would then fuse it to my soul.

As the deep healing sessions were ending for the season, one session had the Holy Ghost's power fall. It was the last one until they started up again a few months later. So much happened at one time...

Gymnasium

"Ok Erin, we will ask the Holy Spirit to bring all the rest of your broken soul parts from middle school in one place to fuse back into your soul."

I got a vision. I was standing in the middle of my school gymnasium. I faced a gym full of my broken soul parts—the bleachers were filled with them! These were all fragmented soul parts from when I was hurt, teased, and misunderstood. They all resembled how I looked in middle school—my high jean pant legs and awkward itchy wigs.

As I told the three women in my session what I saw, one woman said, "Holy Spirit, can you bring all these broken soul parts into Erin's growing and maturing soul?"

When she said this, my broken soul parts began to form lines, walking down the bleacher steps, lining up, and making their way down to the middle of the gym. I saw my current maturing soul standing in a glowing light. One by one, each soul part walked into my soul and became whole. I saw the excitement in the room. There was a vibrating energy. These fragmented soul parts no longer had to be separated and in pain. I was becoming whole by the power of God.

The Beauty in Restoration

"When you have clung to Jesus through pain and problems and experienced his amazing grace, you find joy in him," Jo Ann Leavell, distinguished minister's wife, and author (1 Sept. 1931 - 6 Mar. 2015).

Japanese art has a tradition of mending broken pottery with gold. This art is called kintsukuroi, "golden repair." The shattered pieces are sealed back together with gold. The history of the broken pieces gives an artistic display, as the gold filling shows the sharp edges and curves. What was once broken has now become whole. The piece of pottery is more beautiful than before. It is unique and one-of-a-kind, as not every piece has been broken the same way.

God's power to make us whole brings the same beauty. He heals us piece by piece. The rigid and rough pieces from our broken past now gather, and the glory of God seals us back together. What the world would discredit as ugly and unrepairable, God sees as a beautiful masterpiece waiting to happen. No person is too broken for God to repair.

Set Apart

Christians make mistakes in the gospel message, such as teaching that everything will immediately be put back together and made whole the moment we are saved. But this is not true. Some Christians find the process quicker, and others may find it slower. It is God's will to heal all of us and make us whole, but the purpose of our lives is the biggest factor in how long that process will take.

I was in my car one afternoon. Frustrated, I began asking God why he didn't heal me immediately from everything. While I prayed, I got a vision of a kitchen counter. There was a glass vase with kitchen tools inside. I saw a hand pull out a large golden spoon. I was reminded of the verse in 2 Timothy 2:20-21 NIV, "In a large house there are articles not only of gold and silver, but also of wood and clay; some are for special purposes and some for common use. Those who cleanse themselves from the latter will be instruments for special purposes, made holy, useful to the Master and prepared to do any good work."

The Holy Spirit then ministered to my heart... *You are the golden spoon. I am going to use you for a special occasion. The ones that get used right away also have a purpose in my Kingdom. They help encourage and strengthen my church.*

In this same encounter, I saw a hand open a drawer full of silverware. This silverware is used every day for eating. Eating every day is vital! In this vision, he was showing me common-use people and special-purpose people.

There seems to be a clash between those used for everyday purposes and those used for special occasions. People can compare their lives to one another and judge based on the path God has called them down individually. One direction doesn't fit all. God's calling for that person is the correct path, although not everyone is just in these two categories. (These are just the two extremes. And everyone in life faces storms. No one is exempt from hardship.)

Common-use people are used more quickly, and they go on to work in ministry and build their family lives and legacy. Special-purpose people usually experience long-drawn-out trials and hardships. When God wants to use that person, he will pull them out, and their calling will start.

"Joseph waited 13 years. Abraham waited 25 years. Moses waited 40 years. Jesus waited 30 years. If God makes you wait, you are in good company."- Anonymous.

These people were separated from the normal for a special purpose in the Kingdom of God. If the journey is longer and harder, then God has a purpose! A verse that's been engraved in my heart is:

Psalm 105:19 NLT
"Until the time came to fulfill his dreams, the LORD tested Joseph's character."

So, what is 40 years to God when preparing a person for a special purpose? Not that long. Forever for us, though!

2 Peter 3:8 ESV
"But do not overlook this one fact, beloved, that with the

Lord one day is as a thousand years, and a thousand years as one day."

Healed, to Wholeness

In Luke 17:11-19, Jesus has mercy on ten lepers. He instructed them to see a priest about their leprosy. As they went, they were healed. One leper came back to Jesus. This leper was overflowing with thankfulness for Jesus healing him. This leper (who was a Samaritan) fell on his face before Jesus and gave God glory.

Luke 17:17-19 (NKJV)
"So Jesus answered and said, 'Were there not ten cleansed? But where are the nine? Were there not any found who returned to give glory to God except this foreigner?' And He said to him, 'Arise, go your way. Your faith has made you well.'"

The last verse in another translation reads, "Thy faith hath made thee *whole*" (KJV). This word "whole" is found in Strong's Greek Lexicon G4982. This word is the Greek word *sōzō*. This same word, *sōzō*, is found throughout scripture interchanging in different translations as saved, whole, healed. Strong's definition is: to save, i.e. deliver or protect (literally or figuratively):—heal, preserve, save (self), do well, be (make) whole.

Ten men were healed, but only one man returned to give God glory. This one man who returned received more than just being cleansed and healed from his leprosy. Now, by Jesus' touch, he was made whole.

I wonder if these nine healed lepers felt some bitterness towards God. They were healed from leprosy, but were they still missing fingers? Did they still have emotional trauma from their years of battling sickness? Their discontent could have been what stopped them from progressing any further. It is enough to give God glory even when everything is still not made right. God still deserves all honor and praise for all he has done. We shouldn't WAIT to honor Him; he deserves all the glory and honor right now.

This lesson has been engraved on my heart. I choose to praise and honor God even with missing hair. I dance for Him while my shaved-bald-spotted head moves around the house. No matter my circumstance, to God have all the honor and praise! What he did for me keeps my thankfulness going. He healed me, cleansed me, and fused my soul back together.

Healing has depths, just as God's Word has an endless depth. The process doesn't end until we are face-to-face with Jesus– when this world fades away and the new has come.

A profound encounter with God changes us. However, it is important to know that a truly radical change can come with pushbacks.

Chapter 11- ENCOUNTER WARS

I have noticed that when a powerful event from God takes place, an opposing force immediately tries to steal the moment. I call these two opposing events _encounter wars_. I'll have a powerful, life-changing encounter with God, only to be faced with the adversary (devil) who tries to steal what has taken place. If he can't steal the miracle, he will try to steal my perception of it.

I experienced the beginning of this when God told me to pray for healing for the brain-dead man. A supernatural miracle took place in that ICU room; God's power filled the atmosphere. As I walked down the hallway after praying, the adversary met me. He tried to steal what had taken place by telling me lies. Threatening me and filling my thoughts with doubt and insecurities.

My second _encounter war_ happened in church. I was at a small church that didn't believe in speaking in tongues around other people. I was sitting in a Wednesday night service when the pastor felt led by God to invite people to come to the front where he could pray for them to be baptized by the Holy Spirit. Walking up, I felt God's nudge on my heart. I could tell he wanted me there.

As the pastor prayed for everyone, I closed my eyes and held out my hands. I decided to pray in tongues but "quietly" under my breath. As he was praying, and I was praying in the spirit, I had a surge of power begin to flow through my body. It felt like a pulsating electrical current. I raised my hands, and my tongues became louder. The intensity of the power grew. I was aware of my surroundings, and although my eyes were closed, I knew the room fell silent. The pastor had stopped praying. I didn't open my eyes; I surrendered to God's power. I wanted to be used by Him in whatever way he wanted. I wanted to surrender to His will. My tongues became even louder and more authoritative. I prayed in English for revival. I heard the pastor on stage begin to speak again; I stopped praying and lowered my head. The surge of power was still flowing through me with my hands up. It felt like I touched an electrical socket, but it wasn't painful.

I raised my hands for what seemed a long time with my eyes still closed. When I finally looked around, I saw that the whole church had left. The pastor said thoughtful words to me, but I could tell he didn't know how to respond. At that moment, I truly believed the pastor and that church didn't really expect a baptism of the Holy Spirit. Like most churches, they just wanted a mediocre prayer– with mediocre results.

God did something so beautiful in that service. I was baptized by the Holy Spirit!

I left the main sanctuary and walked to the youth building to pick up my daughter. It was then that I had my opposing *encounter*. A few church members gave me dirty looks as I walked past them. Some people, when they saw me, would look the other way so they wouldn't have to speak to me. One older blonde lady deliberately gave me a dirty look as if

I had done something wrong.

I was faced with an empty building and dirty looks from so-called Christians. There was a knot in my stomach. My thoughts flooded with: *Did I do something wrong? I should have prayed quietly. I shouldn't have prayed in tongues. Was that my boastful flesh, or was it the Holy Spirit leading?*

A third *encounter war* happened two years later when God called me to another fast. This fast was the hardest; I didn't understand why, but I fought through it. I was sick in bed for three days, and I had to transition to juice and soft liquid foods to finish the fast. My sister invited me to a healing/deliverance service. I took my daughter with me as well.

It was an evening service. The event started with worship, which then proceeded to a Bible teaching about the woman who touched Jesus' garment. After the message, there was an open invitation to come to the front to get prayed for. One at a time, people were coming up. A couple of people were delivered from demons. I felt a pounding in my heart, and I knew God was pushing me forward. As I approached the front, the woman there inquired about my prayer needs. As I was talking, I saw someone walking up from the corner of my eye. As my head turned, I noticed that it was my daughter. She was crying, and her shoulder muscles were tense. God had nudged at her heart to come up, too.

A deliverance session took place for my daughter and me. A familiar/generational spirit attacked both our bloodlines. Miraculously, both of us were delivered. A prophecy followed the deliverance, and this prophecy is coming to pass in many ways, even as I write this book. God moved, God delivered, God spoke.

Feeling tired and weak, I sat down in the back where our seats were. A male pastor who witnessed the deliverance from his seat joined us and started a conversation. We moved to a back room to continue talking so we wouldn't disturb the rest of the people praying. My sister, my daughter, and I engaged in what I thought would be a wholesome Christian conversation. I told this pastor I was on Day 16 of my fast. He frowned at me and said, "God didn't tell you to fast." He then tried to lecture me that Christians don't fast anymore. He was arguing that fasting is an Old Testament practice. As this man was talking (and becoming angry with me), the Holy Spirit began speaking inside my heart— *"Jesus says when we fast"*... *"Some only come out by prayer and fasting"*... (Matt. 6:16, Mark 9:29). These are Bible verses that encourage New Testament Christians to fast.

This pastor became argumentative with me, and I left without trying to resolve anything. I knew by this time what the enemy was doing. And I wouldn't let him steal my focus on what God had just done. God delivered me and my daughter that night! And the devil was mad.

I began to speak out loud about how amazing God was. Driving home, I continued to declare God's goodness and recap all that had happened—from God, NOT from the enemy. I kept testifying to what God had done. It was then that my daughter caught on and was excited once again. *Yes, God did something great.*

The greater the power, the greater the potential war. Standing on the Word of God and the history built with God will help if the enemy comes. There truly is a spiritual war, and it's a season when we must be strong.

Elijah, the prophet from the Old Testament, had his own *encounter wars*. He had supernatural faith to go against hundreds of false prophets. He had extreme faith to call down fire from Heaven to consume watered-down wood. As Elijah left that place after the crazy signs and wonders, he was faced with his adversary, the devil, in the form of Jezebel. Jezebel threatened to kill Elijah, and he ran for his life (1 Kings 18 & 19).

Jesus had *encounter wars* when he healed certain people. At times, after the healing miracles had taken place, an angry mob would surround him and yell at him. He was forced out of cities. I can't help but imagine a grin on Jesus' face as he left. Something incredible happened, and the devil couldn't do anything about that moment. He could only try to throw a tantrum after the fact.

Is it worth the fight? Encountering God and living with the results of what God has done... I can be a first-hand witness to say, "It is worth it!" A change happened. Healing took place at some level. Demonic chains were loosened or even broken and completely cut off.

God *encounters* are always worth it. Whatever God has planned, however hard it may be, trust that His ways are good. Good doesn't necessarily mean comfort. Good doesn't mean success and riches in our worldly eyes. Good is defined by God.

Isaiah 55:8 NIV
"For my thoughts are not your thoughts, neither are your ways my ways,' declares the LORD."

Through this journey, God taught me to ask, "Is this the distraction?" We are not to dwell on the enemy's works, although we can learn from them. But there are other times when even speaking about the attack is not God's will. It puts more attention on evil than the miracle that has just taken place. I'm not talking about dismissing the discussion of spiritual warfare. However, wisdom is needed if God has done something great and the enemy has his own encounter set against what God has done. Great Elijah moments can come at a great price. If we are not grounded and strong in the Word, we can be swept away by our adversary.

Translucent Life

Soaking on this concept of Elijah moments, I get a vision: I see myself standing, appearing "see-through." A hand moves through me to show how transparent I have become. I look like a ghost. I hear the Lord saying to me while I see this vision, "You have become translucent." He tells me he made me this way so people can easily see me as vulnerable—to see my heart and flaws. But I see my flaws covered in the glory of God. As I still soak in this vision, I see butterflies fly off of me as the Lord speaks, "You are a new creation."

A depth of power was being made available. The more significant cost I have experienced is the humility needed to hold what He gave me—to show the world my vulnerability and God's power at the same time.

When a TRUE God encounter occurs, the atmosphere shifts, and God's original beauty and design can function again. God creates beautiful things.

Chapter 12- HANDS THAT BUILD

The more breakthroughs I experienced, the easier it was to hear God. My relationship with Him got sweeter, even though I had my struggles.

I began to get visions of God's hands doing things while I prayed over people. I saw God's hands performing what looked like surgery for one man. God opened his stomach, and a dark cloud flew out. Then, the hands sowed the stomach back up.

I prayed for a friend who was battling abdominal pain. As I prayed for intercession and healing over her body, I saw God's hand moving swiftly through her. She contacted me later that day and said she had a breakthrough after experiencing God move through her, and she felt lighter. She said the pain was gone. God's hands did work on her behalf. And he healed her.

I am reminded of the passage where Jesus says he only does what he sees His Father doing (John 5:19). The Bible describes hands many times. Hands represent work that is being created and fashioned. Our hands build and create things. People can build and make things with other resources, but it's the concept that a person is doing something. God wants our hands to be blessed, our works on earth to be beautiful and impactful, and our hands to be like his.

I want your hands to build and not destroy, Erin.

God was calling me to a life higher than my own—a life of beauty and purpose, a life filled with God's goodness and glory, a life that isn't overtaken by darkness. I was looking at the sunset one evening as I pondered this concept. God created the heavens and the earth, and he made the beautiful sunset with his hands. God's handiwork is beautiful.

Psalm 19:1 NIV
"The heavens declare the glory of God; the skies proclaim the work of his hands."

There was a struggle in my heart. Shouldn't I be completely healed before helping others around me? Although the intensity of hair-pulling had lessened tremendously, and I was not trapped in endless cycles like I used to, I still slipped into pulling occasionally.

God used me to pray for the brain-dead man in the hospital. I was a mess when he chose me. I wonder how many people were in that hospital. How many people did he glance through at the church who were praying for the man? What made him choose the girl who pulled out her hair?

God's ways and his thoughts are higher than ours. He is always working. His works may seem behind the scenes—unknown and unseen to us who are desperately trying to understand. But... he is a good Father, and he has good plans.

Purple Gem

I was in a prayer Zoom meeting that lasted all day. It was around midnight, and I was sitting on the ground to keep my phone plugged into the wall while praying. I was getting tired and felt like I was wrapping up my prayers for the evening. While praying in tongues, I saw a large, bright purple gem inside my stomach. I asked the group what they thought it meant. I received a prophetic word: "A royal anointing was going to flow from your belly as streams of living water." The color purple represents royalty. One verse was given to me.

2 Corinthians 3:18 NLT
"So all of us who have had that veil removed can see and reflect the glory of the Lord. And the Lord—who is the Spirit—makes us more and more like him as we are changed into his glorious image."

I stored this vision in my heart.

One month later, I was at a Christian family camp with my daughter. The kids had their fun day while the adults gathered for a Bible Study. The pastor leading the lesson was from Focus on the Family ministry. They focused on strengthening marriages for stronger families. As I was a single mom, this lesson was especially hard for me.

The pastor's name was Greg. He held up a large fake diamond in his hand. He taught us to admire the flaws and beauty of the diamond. He related a wife to being a husband's diamond. The lesson turned into an exercise as the men faced their wives to tell them how beautiful they were. My heart sank. I was alone. And the life of being a single mom taunted me all week staying there. This day intensified my husbandless life.

The invitation to feel alone and unloved tried to return to my emotions. I sat there quietly as I heard the voices of all participating in the exercise. I then felt God's presence cover me like a warm blanket and he said, "You are my diamond." He brought me back to my vision while praying on my hardwood floor—the vision of the large purple diamond in my belly. The overall meaning now came to life. I am God's diamond.

Bible verses flooded my thoughts as I felt the warmth of his presence. "When my father and my mother forsake me, then the Lord will take care of me" (Psalm 27:10 NKJV). "The Lord is close to the brokenhearted and saves those who are crushed in spirit" (Psalm 34:18 NIV).

There were other hardships in my life, but hair-pulling was the highlight of this book. God's truth and love have been carried into every broken piece of me, and he turns it into His beautiful love story.

You may not relate to hair-pulling, but there may be a brokenness inside you, a struggle you are facing that seems to have no end. God understands your pain. He understands your shame. If you give your healing journey to Him, He can change the script. He can rewrite your past. He can change your future. He can love you through the process. Your healing can happen piece by piece, moment by moment. Or all at one time. His choosing. His timing. His ways.

Hidden Gems

What does God say about YOU in this hour? God says: My people must hear that I am a good Father. I am calling out to my hidden ones in this hour– the ones I have purposely hidden. These hidden ones have been through great trials and tribulations. The time it took to make you was long and tiresome. But you made it, says the Lord; you weathered the storm beatings. You are in this hour of time to represent my glory, to represent me. With this great glory comes great testing. Otherwise, you never would be able to make it. You would burst. The best wine calls for the toughest and thickest wineskins. My glory is coming; do you see it? My glory is coming; do you feel it? Breathe it in, my child. It is for you to spread like wildfire. I love you, says the Lord.

Chapter 13- TWENTY-NINE

The number 29 isn't usually a number that stands out. Twenty-nine is in that awkward stage of becoming a better number, like 30— on the other end next to the not-so-important number 28. Yet, if God highlights it, it is a profound number in the spiritual realm. As I write this last chapter, God has been highlighting the number 29 to me. It is the 29th year I have been battling pulling out my hair. The number 29 has been repeated as if it were a repetitious hammer. Twenty-nine. Twenty-nine. Twenty-nine.

Another way he has been showing me was through my music. Spotify generates a summary of the music most played and top artists for the listener. Having a teenager, I hear a lot about this end-of-year report. I never cared to look into it, but I felt led to this time. As I got my end-of-year 2024 report, the top song of the year for me was Dunamis by Mercy Culture. As I glanced at the number of times I listened to this song, it was twenty-nine times.

Some music lovers probably listen to their favorite song more than that. But I felt God's nudge on my heart as I saw that number. He was speaking, and it is important to listen.

Dunamis is a Greek word found in the Bible. It means power, strength, ability, might, and miracle. Dunamis means God's power flowing through a person. God's dunamis power has been documented in scripture by how Jesus performed miracles. The woman with the issue of blood for twelve years was healed by the dunamis power flowing from Jesus.

Mark 5:30 NIV
"At once Jesus realized that power [dunamis] had gone out from him. He turned around in the crowd and asked, 'Who touched my clothes?'"

God has paired the number twenty-nine with his dunamis power. Both have been on my heart as I write this chapter.

Troy Brewer is well-known for his book "Numbers That Preach." In this book, he explains in detail what the number twenty-nine is. The number twenty-nine can represent mountains. There are twenty-nine mountains in the Bible. Mountains in the Bible have been known to be a place where God's prophets journey. Once they reach the mountain, it has been a place where they hear God's voice. Mountains are a place for hearing God's voice and getting instructions.

Twenty-nine can also mean departure. Pastor Troy Brewer's website (www.troybrewer.com) gives details on this revelation:

"This being the last number of the series of twenties, it depicts a change from the covering of one's house into something new. Also, because the number nine has to do with the judgment of the Holy Spirit, the baptism of fire, it is preparatory to the number thirty, which is about dedication to rulership."

The twenty-ninth time the name Noah was used in the Bible was when the flood waters resided, and the people departed from the ark.

Genesis 8:18-19 NIV
"So Noah came out, together with his sons and his wife and his sons' wives. All the animals and all the creatures that move along the ground and all the birds—everything that moves on land—came out of the ark, one kind after another."

There is a list of other people whose names have been mentioned in the Bible for the 29th time who have departed from something. Joshua's name stood out to me. The twenty-ninth time his name is mentioned in the Bible is when he was preparing the Israelites to leave the wilderness into their promised land (Joshua 1:12).

I feel a shift in my season of life—a change from where I've been into something new. The biggest shift is the moment of publishing this book. Whatever may come of this, my prayers are that the individual reading can experience Jesus in deeper ways. Jesus hung on that cross, thinking of you. There is nothing he cannot understand about the life you have been living. There's power in repenting and renouncing sins. Your healing may come all at once, or little by little.

God's ways are always good when we surrender to Him. God has a plan and a purpose that is unique to each person. A person's healing journey is special to the Lord.

My healing comes in time, but with great purpose, says the Lord. You were never meant to be like everyone else. You were meant to stand out. You were meant to be unique. You were meant to reflect my GLORY. My glory is flowing all around you now. It is time to step out into the greatness for which I have destined you— not for your own pleasures or glory, but for My glory. My healing comes in time, but what an impact it has on your character and perseverance in the waiting. The true miracle is who you become in the journey. We are one together. Let this unity we share be a weapon used to destroy darkness, to destroy all the enemy has built up. Light up the world, my child. It is now your time to shine. Shine bright for me! - God

THE TRUE MIRACLE IS WHO YOU BECOME IN THE JOURNEY.

Pride and Prejudice

I love to watch Pride and Prejudice. I enjoy the 2005 version, played by Keira Knightly and Matthew Macfadyen. God speaks to me while I watch it, and I feel an awe-inspiring love that flows through me as the storyline unfolds. The Holy Spirit ministers to my heart.

Mr. Darcy (cast by Matthew Macfadyen) does many things for this woman behind the scenes, even though his efforts are unseen by many. He makes things right, respects her, and loves her purely.

The movie's ending unfolds when Elizabeth Bennet (played by Keira Knightly) has a sleepless night longing for Mr. Darcy. She is now aware of his passionate love for her and his desire to marry her. She steps outside to go for a morning walk at the break of dawn. Mist is still on the blades of grass as the sun is slowly rising. And she sees him with the glowing light behind him— making his way to her. He couldn't sleep either. Their thoughts were for each other. The moment happens when their steps stop as they come face-to-face. They know their love for one another and never have to be without it again.

I always felt God's love surround me while watching the movie. God shows certain characteristics that reflect His love for us. There is a love I can grasp while watching how Mr.

Darcy treats Elizabeth: His love is pure; he does not demand anything in return. His love does not demand a compromise in the woman's purity. His love was working behind the scenes.

Dream: Pink Dressed Lady

I was facing a large green grass field. Music was playing as I soaked up the scene I was in (this was the theme song from Pride and Prejudice). I saw ahead of me, in the middle of the field, Jesus. He was in a gentlemen's suit, his hair pulled back in a low ponytail. I took a look around where I was standing.

I glanced down at my outfit—a pink dress. The music was still playing, and I looked back at Jesus. There was a large tree and a large pool of water beside him. The water was elevated above the ground, and it looked like a large bubble of water. Jesus stretched out his hand. I noticed I could see him so clearly. I saw his face. Jesus smiled at me. With his outstretched hand he said, "Come, Come."

I walked towards him. I glanced at myself in the water. I saw my reflection. I noticed he didn't change anything about me. In my dream, I said, "He must love me just the way I am."

His Face

This was the first time I had ever seen Jesus' face. He chose to reveal himself to me by dressing up in the theme of the Pride and Prejudice movie. Jesus' love is pure. His love flows into each of our lives. He is working behind the scenes.

The color pink represents purity and innocence. Jesus clothed me in this color, although I have fallen in sin and struggled with so much. Jesus' blood speaks louder; he cleanses me from all unrighteousness.

Matthew 5:8 (KJV)
"Blessed are the pure in heart: for they shall see God."

This inner healing and deliverance journey is never in vain. Whatever path God leads us down, he has a plan and a purpose. God can redeem and restore everything.

There is more to this life than just what we think. The greatest gift isn't the healing. The greatest gift is Jesus and who we become in the end. What is in our hearts is so important. The purity of one's heart gives the opportunity to see God. What other joy and fulfillment is there in life?

Jesus is the greatest reward. All else falls short. Healing is easy for God to do. It is us who need to lay down our desires, idols, demons, and flesh… so that God can fill us up with his glorious light. We are meant to reflect God's glory. God's divine power is supposed to flow freely through us to reach a lost and broken world.

May your light shine bright for him. May you put down the ways of this world and do whatever God wants in your life. And may you receive one of the greatest joys— seeing Him face-to-face. May all this be done in His choosing, in His timing, in His ways.

ABOUT THE AUTHOR

Erin May has worked in the medical field for over 18 years. She was born and raised in Beaumont, California, which is nestled between two beautiful mountains. God transitioned her to move to Mansfield, Texas, where she currently lives with her teen daughter. She enjoys soft piano music and hot vanilla cappuccinos. Her studying credentials come from the Holy Spirit, where she has spent endless hours soaking in God's presence.

"Indeed we count them blessed who endure. You have heard of the perseverance of Job and seen the end intended by the Lord- that the Lord is very compassionate and merciful."

James 5:11

CHAPTER 1
REFLECT

Do you believe God still heals today?

_____

_____

_____

_____

Has there been a time you saw God move in someone
else's life, but not your own?

_____

_____

_____

_____

Has God ever told you to do something? What
happened?

_____

_____

_____

_____

CHAPTER 2
REFLECT

Have you ever been hurt by others when you were a child?

How did your past hurts affect your life?

Do you feel seen by God in those hurtful memories?

CHAPTER 3
REFLECT

Reflecting on Ephesians 4:31-32, what stands out to you?

_____

_____

_____

_____

Do you struggle with bitterness?

_____

_____

_____

_____

What is one area of your life you can work on getting better, not bitter?

_____

_____

_____

_____

CHAPTER 4
REFLECT

Is there something you're struggling with that you
thought would go away with age?

Have you ever prayed for God to heal you? Estimate
how many times?

How do you invision God's healing touch in your life?
How do you expect God to heal you?

CHAPTER 5
REFLECT

Do you have any hidden sins that need to be brought to the light? (1 John 1:9, James 5:16)

_____

_____

_____

_____

What is your understanding of repenting and renouncing of past sins/generational sins? (Proverbs 28:13)

_____

_____

_____

_____

Are you afraid of the supernatural realm? If so, why?

_____

_____

_____

_____

CHAPTER 6
REFLECT

Take a moment to reflect on words/phrases in your life
that changed the way you live today. Write them down.

_____

_____

_____

_____

Are there painful memories from your past? What are
they?

_____

_____

_____

Jesus understands you, he sees you… Do you believe?

_____

_____

_____

_____

CHAPTER 7
REFLECT

Ask God to help reveal any hidden pride in your life.

_____

_____

_____

_____

Are there people you need to forgive? Write their names down.

_____

_____

_____

_____

Pick one person from above, write **3** good things about this person.

_____

_____

_____

_____

CHAPTER 8
REFLECT

Practice your own 20/20 Bible reading session. Write down one thing God highlighted to you.

Do you have a spiritual gift from God? If not, what gifts do you desire?

What parts of the Bible are you having difficulty believing?

CHAPTER 9
REFLECT

Why are demons considered robbers?

God heals in his choosing, his timing, his ways. Find 3 examples in the Bible of Jesus healing. Then compare/contrast.

Read through Ezekiel Ch. 8. What does Ezekiel find?

CHAPTER 10
REFLECT

Do you consider yourself a "common-use" or "special-purpose" individual?

_____

_____

_____

_____

Is there a past (hurtful) memory that invades your thinking on a regular basis?

_____

_____

_____

_____

Ask for help from God in healing this soul wound. Create your own prayer below.

_____

_____

_____

_____

CHAPTER 11
REFLECT

Why do you think a great encounter with God has a higher risk for spiritual warfare?

_____

_____

_____

_____

Why was Elijah afraid for his life after such an amazing experience of miracles, signs, and wonders? (1 Kings 18 & 19)

_____

_____

_____

_____

Look up Proverbs 3:5-6. Write passage below.

_____

_____

_____

_____

CHAPTER 12
REFLECT

Do you struggle with something that is hard to overcome?

What are things you can create that are beautiful and purposeful?

Have you personally encountered Jesus while reading this book? What happened?

CHAPTER 13
REFLECT

Ask God to reveal an area of your life that you need to
surrender to Him.

How can you begin your personal healing journey
today? (Or continue)

What has inspired you about this book?

MY NOTES

www.ingramcontent.com/pod-product-compliance
Lightning Source LLC
Chambersburg PA
CBHW061651120626
46550CB00003B/908